WAKE ME UP!

A True Story

WAKE *ME* UP!

"This true story of a love lost to violence proves that love is never lost, and that life continues past the point we refer to as death. Lyn discovers the truth of Chip's survival on the other side and takes us along on her journey of awakening. The story is riveting. I found it impossible to put down. Lyn came through the disbelief and grief of having the love of her life snatched from her and has written the story of her transformation to assist others going through similar circumstances. She shows courage and strength on every page."

—Linda Moore, Author of *Memories of Magdalene*

"Lyn writes a story that is both heartbreakingly sad and beautifully validating. What I loved about reading her book is that it came from her own experiences—it validated things I experienced since my husband's death. I have read many books about the Afterlife, but this is the first one where I truly felt validated. Not only was it her truth, it was mine too. I completely identified with *Wake Me Up!*"

—Lynda Matthews, Author of *A Breath Away*

"*Wake Me Up!* is one of the most riveting accounts of Afterlife communication ever written. As an Intuitive and Medium, I receive messages and signs from crossed over spirits daily—but this is stunning. It kept me on the edge of my seat. You will cry, laugh and have your heart filled with the wonder and enchantment of life on the other side."

—Leslie Dutton, *Intuitive & Medium,* Scarborough, Maine

WAKE ME UP!

How Chip's Afterlife Saved Me From Myself

LYN RAGAN

WAKE ME UP!
How Chip's Afterlife Saved Me From Myself
Cover Vision: *Chip Oney*
Interior and Cover Design: by *Lyn Ragan*
Cover Photo © CanStockPhoto, Inc.
Edited by *Marley Gibson*

Trade paper ISBN: 978-0-9916414-0-6
e-Book ISBN: 294-0-0115269-2-3

Any Internet references contained in the work are current at publication time, but Lyn Ragan cannot guarantee that a specific location will continue to be maintained.

Lyn Ragan
Atlanta, GA
info@lynragan.com
www.LynRagan.com

Printed in the United States of America

"For my husband…"

Christopher "Chip" Oney
5/5/1966 - 1/23/2008

Contents

Contents Continued

Acknowledgments

A big thank you to my talented and creative editor, *Author and Freelance Editor*, Marley Gibson (Burns). Endless gratitude to my book angels: Leslie Dutton, Linda Moore, Robert Sharpe, Lynda Matthews, and Margaret Gomez.

Deepest gratitude to Charline, the woman who gave birth to the *love of my life*. If it weren't for her gift of this one beautiful soul, my life would have remained unchanged.

Special thanks to the woman who helped me amend my views and guided me to question my world—Megan Riley. Her gifts are tremendous. "Without you, I know not where I would be."

Greatest of blessings to my beautiful and eccentric mom, my guiding light. I wouldn't be who I am today without her. "I thank you for giving me life and loving me throughout."

And to my beautiful sister, Deb. Words will never describe the appreciation I have for this beautiful woman. She's my rock, my best friend—I love her more than she'll ever know. "What a blessing to be sharing this life with you."

Without Chip, there'd be no story to share. His beautiful love is truly a divine gift. How lucky am I to have shared an enormous chapter of my life with Chip not only in the physical, but from this other place called *The Afterlife* as well. Words can't begin to describe my gratefulness…

Until we arrive in each others arms once more…
I will love you always.

Other Books By Lyn Ragan

WE NEED TO TALK
Living With The Afterlife

SIGNS FROM THE AFTERLIFE
Identifying Gifts From The Other Side

SIGNS FROM PETS IN THE AFTERLIFE
Identifying Messages From Pets in Heaven

BERC'S INNER VOICE
(Children's Book)
Author, Lyn Ragan
Illustrator, Alison Meyer

T his is a true story. Some names, places, and other identifying details were changed to protect a murder investigation and individual privacy. The timing of events was compressed to facilitate the telling of the story.

No part of this book is intended for educational purposes. This story is about this author's personal experiences. Please keep in mind that no two people experience the same communications—they are as individual as humans are.

Chapter One

THE CAUSE OF THE PAIN

JANUARY 23, 2008

I would have never thought it. Not in a million years. To wake up to the sound of love, only to experience unspeakable tragedy minutes later… it was clearly a day that would change our lives forever.

At 4:33 a.m. my phone rang. Startled, I shot out of bed. I was always up by four o'clock, but today, I was late. The phone was sitting on a table across the room. I ran over to pick it up and then answered, sweetly.

"Good morning, my sweetie pie."

"Good morning, baby doll," my lover said, enthusiastically.

I adored our early morning calls; my daily dose of love.

While I pretended to be up a few minutes prior to him calling, I moved through the house to let the fur-kids out to potty. I walked outside, watched our dogs do their duties, and while my sweetheart talked about the night before, I marched back inside.

Chip was sharing how bad he felt. Because of his irritating cough, he said he wasn't able to get much sleep. Meanwhile, I brought down one of our new cups he insisted we buy for Christmas. I placed it on the counter next to the coffee pot, turned it on and waited for the brewing to end.

We were both fighting a terrible cold. Chip had an early day at work planned. Yesterday, we decided to take some time off to play. I would leave work at noon, meet him at home, we'd hop in the new car we bought last week, and go for a ride.

"That'll make us feel better," he said. But today, he doesn't sound so good. In fact, he sounded horrible.

"You're probably not going to feel like going later, are you?" I asked him. I thought he might say no, so I was surprised when he replied, "Let's wait to see how I feel when that time gets here, okay?"

As we talked on his way to work, I pictured him perfectly sitting in the driver's seat of his big red Dually Dodge. I knew he was holding his maroon Starbucks coffee mug in his right hand, while resting his arm on the middle console. His left hand was hanging over the top of the steering wheel while he talked through the Bluetooth connected to his left ear.

I didn't hear him stop to unlock the gate. Nor did I hear him take the cooler from his pickup and put it into his semi. What I did hear—was him starting the big truck. I heard the sound of the engine turn over and I knew with certainty I said, "I heard you start her up, sweetie."

"Yep, we started her up," I know he replied.

I then pictured him hopping down out of the semi needing to start his pre-trip inspection. He never skipped that part of his routine. But on this one morning, he only took one or two steps forward before our lives changed forever.

At this moment in time, I knew nothing.

Once I heard the truck start, I imagined him still sitting inside realizing something went wrong. The reason I assumed this was that only seconds later, at approximately 4:45 a.m., his voice growled out two big words.

"Oh shit!"

I instantly thought something wasn't quite right with the truck and I asked, "What's wrong, sweetie?"

But he didn't reply.

I then pictured him getting out of the truck to check the engine. I knew that was the first place he'd go. He'd have to release the latches on each side of the hood in order to lift it.

But how did he do that so fast?

What I heard next was a horrific, loud sound blasting through the phone. So much so that I had to take it away from my ear. I couldn't hear anything but a horrible noise that sounded like a lawnmower engine. It was deafening. It was difficult to fathom anything under the hood being that loud, but again, I still didn't know anything.

I asked once again, "Sweetie, what's wrong with the truck?"

How can he hear me if I can't hear him?

Through the loud noise though, I continued to ask, shouting now. "Chip, can you hear me?"

Something felt so wrong. As I paced back and forth in my living room, I decided he needed my help. I ran into the kitchen and grabbed my keys off the counter. At that exact moment, the sound of the lawnmower engine slowly tempered off.

"Sweetie, is everything all right? Are you okay?"

But I got nothing back.

Suddenly, I heard what I thought was Chip sniffling. I knew then he was still on the phone.

Why isn't he talking to me? Is he playing a bad game?

I asked yet again, "Sweetie pie, are you all right?"

No words came through my ear.

I charged out the front door, leaving the dogs in the house, and raced to my car. I listened intently for anything he might say. At the same time I reassured him I was on my way to help him. I lived less than two miles from where he parked; it wouldn't take me long to get there.

"I'm on my way, sweetie. I don't know what's wrong, but I'm coming to help, okay? You're not talking to me darlin', and you're starting to scare me."

I could hear him breathing, but he never said a word.

"Are you okay, sweetie?"

I flew down Normandy Boulevard hitting seventy-five and eighty miles per hour in a thirty mile per hour zone. It never dawned on me to slow down.

"You need to say something, darlin'. Why aren't you talking to me, Chip?" My heart was racing now and my legs were shaking uncontrollably. Fear had creeped in.

There was a lot of traffic out to be so early in the morning. At one point, I got stuck at a red light where I sat behind a white work truck listening to Chip's breathing in my ear. My mind was racing wild fast.

"Sweetie, do I need to hang up and call 911? Can you talk to me? You're scaring me, Chip. I don't know what's wrong. Please say something to me. Please, Chip, say anything."

Still, no words echoed through my ear.

"As soon as I get around this truck I'm there, sweetie."

I sped through the last light before arriving at the lot.

"I'm right here, darlin'. I'm turning into the driveway right now, coming to you. I am right here!"

I saw the lights shining across the lot from his truck. The driveway was bumpy as I passed the office buildings on the main road. It was so damn *dark* out.

"I'm here, sweetie. Where are you?"

And then, my eyes found him. I could see him off in the distance lying on the ground next to his truck.

"Oh my God, oh my God!" I yelled.

I heard those words flying all around my head in the thick

air, over and over again. They had nowhere to escape.

My foot stomped the gas pedal as I rushed to his side.

I stopped not directly in front of him, but more off to the right. When I slammed the car into park and sought for him to move, I noticed streaks of blood running across his forehead. I knew I had to get help fast. I jumped out and ran toward the road. But then I thought, *is he still alive?*

I turned around and ran back. I searched to see if his chest was moving up and down.

Oh, thank God, he's alive!

Disturbingly though, I saw a large hole in the back of his head. I rapidly concluded that he must have fallen off of the truck somehow and hurt himself. There was so much blood.

I knew I had to calm myself down and shut off my thoughts. It was imperative I help him. Getting off the phone was the first step.

"I have to hang up now, sweetie, so I can call 911. I'll be right back. Okay? I promise!"

I hit the end button and disconnected us. I saw the blue light blink twice by his head, glowing brightly through the darkness. He could no longer hear my voice and that worried me.

I turned and ran as fast as I could. It was vital I had the physical address to get help, fast. At the same time I dialed.

4:53 a.m. — I pressed 911, but it didn't go through. I tried again, but got nothing. I called "0," and again, I got no tone whatsoever.

4:54 a.m. — I dialed 411. I gave city and state information. An operator answered. I told her I needed 911, but now she was gone, too. It felt like a lifetime before a voice answered I was unable to register.

I had long reached the road and was waiting in front of the mailbox, staring directly at the property numbers.

I shouted, "Is this 911?"

She responded, "Yes."

Instantly, I yelled it out.

"I need an ambulance at 9501 Normandy Boulevard."

I repeated it two more times with complete verbal accuracy and no southern drawl. I insisted on having no mental errors. There could be no mistakes.

I remember the 911 operator asking me questions about my relationship with Chip and after I answered, I made sure to tell her about the large hole in the back of his head.

In my fogginess, all I could think about was how we needed help immediately. I don't think I said it out loud, though. And then, out of nowhere, she put a man on the phone.

He asked if Chip was still breathing.

"I don't know," I told him. "I came out here to the road to get the address. I'm going back right now."

I ran to Chip as quickly as I could. While I was running, I glanced at his truck. The hood wasn't raised. It was intact as though nothing had been touched.

Why didn't I see that before?

I hurriedly tried to piece it all together.

So he didn't go under the hood? What was that noise then? How'd he get hurt? He must've fallen off the truck and hit something. *That's it, he fell.*

Once I was beside him, I repeated it again to the 911 operator. "He has a large hole in the back of his head."

His head was resting in a mud puddle combined with a large amount of his blood. I couldn't tell if it was brain matter or if it was bone lying right underneath his head. I walked around him and squatted on the left side of his body. I stared at his face noting how calm he appeared and then I watched him breathe.

His chest moved up and then slowly down. He appeared to

be asleep, yet snoring loudly. I'd watched him sleep many times before—it was exactly how he looked now.

There were streaks of blood that made crisscross marks across the top of his head.

How did you get these blood marks, Chip? They're odd. And I don't see anything else on your face.

I'd mentioned Chip's snoring to the man on the phone. He told me he was gasping for air.

And then he said, "I'm going to tell you what you need to do to help him breathe easier until help arrives. I will instruct you step-by-step."

First, he said I'd have to lift Chip's head back by placing my hand under his neck. I did. I buried my hand in the mud and pushed as far as I could under his neck, and then I tried to lift him.

He didn't move. I couldn't budge him. He was so heavy. The man told me again I needed to lift his head back to open his airways, so I kept trying.

I placed my phone on top of his stomach and I positioned myself above him with my hands under his neck. With both hands now locked, I lifted with all my might.

I still couldn't move him. His head seemed to be stuck in the mud.

I picked up the phone and asked the stranger a question.

"Are you sure you want me to do this when the hole on the back of his head is so big?" I was terrified I'd make it worse for Chip and cause him to lose blood faster.

I don't think the man replied to my question, or either I don't remember what he said. The next thing I heard was him telling me I needed to clean out Chip's mouth so he wouldn't choke on anything.

By this time, my hands were downright muddy. The only

thing I could think of was putting all that mud inside of his mouth. I wiped my hands on my clothes and tried to clean them as much as possible.

I leaned forward, closer to his face, and right when I was about to open his mouth, he took a breath. He scared me and I leaped back.

God, I can't put my filthy fingers in his mouth. I can't make this worse for him than everything already is.

I knew he was breathing because I was sitting there watching him. But I felt totally helpless. I couldn't lift him; he weighed two hundred and twenty-five pounds and was almost double my size. I couldn't budge him, his head wouldn't move.

I was so scared—for him.

"When are they going to be here?" I hollered at the phone.

"They're on the way," the man shouted back.

And then it hit me.

They won't see us! Not back here in this darkness.

I jumped up and ran back to the road.

(If you can picture the size of a football field, imagine me located at the one yard line standing on Normandy while Chip is located at the fifty.)

Everything felt like it was taking forever.

I paced back and forth on the dark road, looking for lights to appear. There were none. It wasn't long before I heard that stranger's voice again. He asked if Chip was still breathing. I had to confess I'd returned to the road to wait for the ambulance.

"You need to help Chip; you need to go back to him," he told me firmly.

I turned and ran. Never questioning if he was right or wrong. *I know they won't see us. It's too dark out.*

But I ran anyway. Chip needed me with him.

I squatted down in the identical spot where I was before.

I laid my hand on top of his tummy; I needed to be touching him. While we waited, this time I looked around. I glanced to the right and peered behind me at the truck.

I saw no blood anywhere on the back of it and I couldn't see where he would have fallen either. There was no disturbance on the ground below or around the immediate area of his truck. I then studied Chip from head to toe, observing him stretched out in front of me.

He was wearing his Gator Football blue and orange sweat shirt with his khaki-colored shorts. I saw his white ankle socks and his dark brown leather work shoes, too. He was lying flat on his back with his legs slightly parted and his arms were out to his side. His coffee mug had fallen out of his hand and it was resting right beside him in the wet grass.

I didn't see anything out of the ordinary. The only lights upon us were the ones from my car headlights and they were sitting at an angle. The moon was bright above us, but it wasn't illuminating enough to see anything clearly.

I watched him sleep. There was nothing else I could do but sit with him in the darkness... and wait. I leaned over and kissed his cheek, his eyes, his head, and I told him I loved him.

I rubbed his cheek with my hand and I begged him, "Just hang on, sweetie, they're on their way. They'll be here soon. Just hang on."

But inside I was screaming it at the top of my lungs, *please hang on, my love! Please don't leave me!*

Lights were beaming through the trees. Finally. They were here. I hollered into the phone. "Tell them to turn now! Make a right-hand turn now or they'll miss our road."

I sat there and watched them drive past us. Another rescue unit went by, and then another. My voice cracked in its determination to control the situation.

"Tell them to make a U-turn and then make another one to come right back here," I screamed.

I could hear the stranger talking, but not to me. I waited for them to return, but they didn't. Too much time had gone by. I realized it then, they didn't make that second U-turn.

"Where are they? They didn't come back," I yelled.

I knew time was critical. I was beyond terrified. This was all taking so long. I knew we were teetering on the edge of saving Chip's life.

I jumped up and ran as fast as I could. It had rained all night long, so I hit every puddle on the dirt road leading back to Normandy. My pajama pants were soaked with mud.

When I reached the highway, I couldn't see a rescue unit anywhere. They were gone. They vanished. The road was pitch-black. It was as though I had closed my eyes and become blind.

I screamed into the phone, "Where are they? Where did they go?"

The stranger's voice wasn't as calm as it was earlier. He convincingly responded, "They're trying to find you!"

"Oh, wait," I shouted. "I can see them."

I saw the lights appearing from a good distance down the road. Before I knew which way they would turn though, I fell.

My knees hit the pavement, hard; they gave out. I found myself praying, begging—desperately pleading—out loud.

"Please tell them to come back this way. Tell them to please, please, please… come back this way."

I could feel the pounding of my heart inside my head now. It was taking everything I had to stay focused.

I watched as the lights slowly crossed the median. *Yes!* They were heading toward us. I counted to three as they all turned in our direction. As calmly as I could, I waited for their arrival.

Right before they reached me though, a police car appeared out of nowhere. It was in the left-hand lane next to the rescue unit leading the way. The flashing neon blue of its lights were reflecting all over the dark. I sensed the speed it was traveling, fast. And when a bright light shined upon me, I couldn't help but wave frantically.

I imagined what they saw: a woman on the side of the road in the middle of nowhere. She had wild hair and mud-covered pajamas, jumping up and down, waving her arms madly.

"This way, this way!" I screamed.

I knew they couldn't hear my pleas for them to hurry. They were still too far away, but I hollered it out anyway.

The first rescue pulled into the driveway. I told them to go straight back to the right side of the lot, and Chip would be on the other side of my car.

"You will see him," I yelled.

I stood stock-still as they one-by-one drove by. I waited until the police car passed, too. I'd forgotten all about the man on the phone when I pulled my cell back to my ear to see if he was still there.

"Hello?"

"Are they there?" the stranger asked, "I want to make sure they're there before we hang up."

I confirmed.

I ran, fast. Back to Chip. It was now 5:10 a.m. There were three rescue units and one police car by his side. My heart was racing so fast from fear, from running; it felt as though it was going to explode out of my chest. I couldn't control my breathing.

But I kept observing. I watched them all around Chip. The police officer walked over and asked me questions about him like his name, phone number, address, etc., for the next few minutes.

I then tried getting closer to see what they were doing, but the officer told me I needed to step back. He then told me they were going to airlift Chip to Shands Hospital.

A few minutes later, I realized I needed to call his mom. At 5:19 a.m. I dialed Chip's house, but his mother didn't answer. At that exact moment, the police officer walked back over.

"How's he doing?" I asked him. "How'd he get hurt?"

He told me Chip was unconscious. But as soon as I understood what he said, I heard him say something else.

"He's been shot."

My knees went weak again and I fell straight to the ground, shrieking out loud. "Shot? How in the hell did he get shot?"

I didn't really expect an explanation from the officer. I was in total disbelief. It didn't feel real.

I had already pressed the button to re-dial and this time Chip's mom answered. Her sleepy voice danced across my ear.

"Char, this is Lyn. Are you awake enough for me to talk to you?"

"Yeah, sweetie. What's wrong?"

I proceeded to tell her the police informed me her son had been shot and she needed to get to the hospital. I stayed on the phone with her until she got dressed.

And then, I moved closer to Chip. Again, the cop told me I needed to step over to my car. So I did.

I watched as they cut his Gator shirt from his chest. He was bare-chested, but thankfully I could see it moving up and down with his breathing. One of the EMTs brought over a stretcher and this was when I noticed their dilemma. They had to figure out a way to move him.

Three men grabbed his feet and yanked him from the puddle

of blood he was in—they tugged and jerked his body so hard, his head bounced high into the air and then hit the ground with a hard thump. My hands immediately clutched the sides of my face when I screamed in silence, "Oh my God, how can they do that? They're hurting him!"

I later learned he was literally stuck in the mud. The first gunshot into his nose sent him sailing straight back. His head sank into the mud bonding him like a suction cup. Brute strength was the only way to pull him out.

I still felt safe in the thought that they were going to take care of him. Silently, I tried to convince myself, "He's in good hands now. They can save him. They will save him!"

The officer took me to his car and told me I needed to sit inside until everything was taken care of. I did as he said. I knew he was tired of telling me to get back. I couldn't blame him. I had no more strength left in me anyway. I was mentally and emotionally spent.

From where I sat inside the police car, I could see Chip perfectly. As they were about to lift him into the rescue, I watched his bare chest continue to move up and down. I could see they had placed an air mask over his face and had put his neck in a brace, too.

The officer told me airlifting Chip to the hospital was a good sign. They have hope they'll be able to save him.

Stay alive, sweetie, I prayed. We'll conquer anything and everything. You just need to stay alive, my darling.

It felt like hours had passed. He needed to get to the hospital and I couldn't figure out why they hadn't left yet. I watched everyone like a hawk.

My mind was racing fast. I had literally hundreds of thoughts flashing all at the same time. I couldn't help it. I was locating answers for Chip. I knew he wasn't going to like having scars.

"It doesn't matter what it looks like, we will make sure we fix it so you don't think it'll be ugly," I talked to him inside my head. "There's no worry there, my love."

I assumed he was going to have bad headaches, too. Hell, he had a hole in the back of his head the size of a silver dollar. But I found an answer for that as well. I imagined myself whispering it into his ear.

"Modern medicine will take care of this also, my love. We will make it through whatever we have to. Keep fighting. I'll be right there by your side the entire way. As soon as they let me out of here, I'm on my way. I promise."

I pressed my hands on the car window and smashed my face against the glass. My eyes attacked the stretcher under his head—it was covered, completely, in red.

He was still losing a lot of blood.

Yet, I still sat there hoping against all hope he'd be okay. He would survive. I knew Chip. He was the perfect portrait of a real fighter.

They lifted him up and pushed him inside the rescue. The doors slammed shut and my heart sank. I watched as they backed up and drove away. I could hear the helicopter off in the distance too. I knew exactly when they flew by. Chip loved helicopters. I couldn't imagine that being his last ride in one. We had so much to look forward to. We had so much more to accomplish in our lives together.

Silence.

That was all that surrounded me now. Two police officers and I sat in this God-forsaken pitch black lot in complete, deep and gloomy silence.

I was confined to the back seat of a police car. I had never felt so alone in all of my life. I was petrified for Chip. I couldn't even think of him not surviving.

"Why are they keeping me here? Why won't they let me go to my fiancé? What about the dogs, are they okay?"

"What about work? What will I say? I didn't lock the front door. What if someone breaks in the house and hurts the dogs? I need to go home. I need to get out of here; I need to be with Chip."

My mind was all over the place.

"God, I pray he's okay. How am I going to find out? I hope Char took her phone with her. Should I call his dad and tell him what happened this morning? No. Char will take care of that. I need to get out of this car. Why are they keeping me here?"

My thoughts continued to ramble in my head.

"Oh hell, they think I did this, don't they? But how can they possibly think I'd have anything to do with shooting him? This man is my entire existence."

"What will I do without him if he dies?"

I prayed out loud, "Oh God, please don't let him die. Please take care of Chip, God. Please don't let this be his time. I beg of you, please don't take Chip from me…please!"

There was no concept of time. I knew I needed to get away soon, though. I wanted Chip to know I was trying to get there as fast as I could. He needed me. I should've been allowed to go with him.

Does he know I'm not there?

Seeing all that blood he lost and watching him breath, I couldn't visualize anything else. And my thoughts, they were on a fast track to nowhere.

"He's been shot. Someone shot Chip. It doesn't make sense. None of this makes sense. It can't be real."

"Someone shot Chip!"

I shook my head hard, trying to figure everything out.

"But I'm here, sitting in this cop car where I shouldn't be. I know this can't be happening. It can't possibly be real. There should be a way to start this day all over."

"Maybe I'm still sleeping and all of this is a bad dream."

I figured Chip's mom would be at the hospital now, so I dialed her cell. All of this had to be a bad dream, a horrible nightmare. It couldn't be real, because the next thing I heard was unimaginable.

"Lyn, no, Chip passed away a few minutes ago. He's gone."

On this damp, dark, dreary, ugly Wednesday morning, our lives changed forever.

The love of my life, Christopher J. Oney, died.

My sweet, sweet Chip … was murdered.

Chapter Two

IMPRISONED

"No, Char, they're wrong! Please tell me they're wrong. It's not true—he's not dead. Right?" It couldn't be true. Chip wasn't dead. She had to be wrong.

"No, Lyn. He's gone."

I collapsed.

Out of nowhere I heard a blood curdling scream. It was me, filling the police car with a most horrific squeal. The phone fell from my hand. All I could do was cry.

"No, he can't be dead. This isn't happening. There's no reason for this man to be dead. I can't believe he's dead!" I cried.

The driver's side door slammed closed hard; the officer left. It was a good thing I supposed. The pain was growing more intense as each second passed and my wails were getting louder.

My mind was racing, but my heart—oh my heart—was shattered. It felt like someone had stepped into my body, pulled it from my chest and propelled it high into the wind, only to vanish into infinite dust.

"He's dead? Yes, he died. But how? How did that happen? Oh my God…Chip is dead," I rocked, in shock.

I cried a dreadful cry.

And then I noticed the strangest thing. I saw me. Somehow, I stood outside the door looking in, watching me. I could see my body crouched sideways in the back seat as I tasted the

salty tears pouring into my mouth. I listened to her thoughts—
they were unbearably sad. She was battling, hard, and failing
miserably trying to believe that her man was dead.

"God didn't save him. He took him away, but why? Why is
this happening? My Chip can't be dead," she cried. "Yes, he's
dead! No—he's not. Lyn, yes, he's gone."

"I'm sorry for your loss," the officer had returned.

I couldn't move. I questioned his words, but I had no
strength inside to say anything back. I was so mad at him. How
dare he make me sit in his car when I should've been allowed
to go with Chip and be with him. I should've been allowed to
say goodbye.

Oh my God... I didn't get to say goodbye!

I slammed my head back hitting the hard plastic seat and
broke down again, into a heart-breaking cry.

Time crept by slowly. Tick, tock. Tick, tock. It was
deafening and wouldn't go away. Just when I was ready to
scream in pain, a voice fluttered in from somewhere far off in
the distance. It scared me and shook me back into reality.

"We're now sitting in a crime scene, Ms. Ragan. The
Homicide detectives have been called out. As soon as they
arrive, they'll need to ask you some questions. It'll be at least
another hour before they get here, okay?"

It was the cop.

He had opened the door and I had turned to look. Squatted
down, we were face to face as he tried talking to me. But I
couldn't talk back. There was nothing inside. I didn't even feel
like me. I was gone. I had vanished somehow and was now this
person who was so freaking unbelievably sad.

It was in that moment I realized something though. I wasn't
allowed out of the car. It clicked, loud. I wasn't going

anywhere. Not home, not to the hospital, not to work, not anywhere.

I was about to cry another storm when I felt a sudden vibration in my hand. It was my phone. Chip's mother was calling me back.

"Where are you?" Char asked.

"I'm still sitting here in the police car. I'm not allowed to leave."

"Why can't they just let you go so you can come to the hospital?" she was crying.

"They won't, Char. I can't leave." I knew she needed me there with her. I wanted to be there. I wanted to be able to make this easier for her. For myself somehow. I could hear her heart breaking into pieces.

This is so horrible! How can this be real?

Time mattered no more. There was nothing to go home to. There was nothing to live for. There was nothing to rush to, not anymore.

All that love? For what? For nothing, that's for what. It was gone. Gone. In a flash, he disappeared. Just like that. No goodbye. No see ya. No nothing. Just gone.

I died with that man. I died with that man.

Still sitting in the cop car, I lifted my aching eyes and stared vacantly out the window. It wasn't a dream. The daylight was peeking through the trees. What couldn't be seen hours ago was surely visible now. But I was imprisoned, unable to do anything except sit and watch.

There were several officers surrounding Chip's truck. Two of them stretched out yellow tape and placed it all around his truck and where he laid on the ground too.

It was official—it was a crime scene.

After their initial introduction, two detectives approached

the car. I was presented with and asked to sign a consent form to allow them to search my vehicle. At that second, I knew they considered me a suspect in the murder of my fiancé. It was too obvious.

I signed the papers instantly. I didn't care if they searched the car. I had nothing to hide. What I wanted to do was scream at them, "I didn't do this to my Chip! You're wasting valuable time!" But I had no energy to utter a single word.

Instead, I pressed my head against the seat and closed my eyes tight. The tears were swimming in again and I had no power to stop them. My mind was raging like a hurricane, whipping me up into a violent storm. My emotions—all over the place.

I still couldn't believe he was dead.

Chip's dead, isn't he, God? He's not here anymore. Someone killed him. But I don't understand why. Why Chip?

He had no enemies. He called everyone he knew his friend. Who would do something like this? And why? Why would anyone want to murder him? I couldn't fathom the amount of hatred someone would bear to want his life to end in such a horrid manner.

Chip lived to dream and to work and enjoy life to the fullest. He had the largest heart of anyone I'd ever known. I watched how he interacted with people; he was the warmest, kindest, the most helpful person I'd ever seen. Sometimes a little too kind.

He served thirteen years in the Navy in Special Operations. He was *The Doc* and thoroughly loved his career. In 2003, he left the Navy and landed a local truck driving job hauling gasoline products. Knowing how much his life was still in danger of explosions, he focused on perfecting his skills; he didn't want to encounter an incident. This was also where we met for the first time. I worked there as the evening dispatcher.

My job status met up with a few changes over the years however. I had worked in transportation all of my adult life and my present employer was no exception. The only difference now was I didn't have to worry with company drivers.

As a matter of fact, I was allowed to be disconnected without any worry whatsoever. All freight was dispatched to independent contractors and/or owner-operators.

The prospect of owning his own business intrigued Chip. Several months went by when the opportunity for him to advance into the flatbed division was a welcomed change. Chip bought his own rig and named his business, *CJO Specialized Transport*.

With great enthusiasm and lots of determination, he started his new job. Chip was one of the best operators we used, setting the standard for how the job was done—he was an absolute perfectionist.

He was incredibly proud of himself; he had every right to be. Only weeks earlier he had said, "For the first time in my life darlin, I feel like I'm doing something that isn't dangerous or that'll end my life with an explosion. How will I ever be able to thank you?"

Our relationship was coming together amazingly well and throughout 2007, we dreamed of a future together. For months, we searched for our perfect first house to purchase.

The car door opened again, bringing me back to the present.

"In a few minutes we're going to move across the lot under the canopy and transfer you to a different car," the officer said.

He also told me TV crews were arriving and they wanted to move me out of the way. They didn't want me on the news. That was good because I didn't want to be on the news either.

Within minutes, the officer drove across the lot and parked

beside another car. He got out, opened the door, and guided me to the alternate vehicle.

I no longer had a front row seat but I could see quite a bit. The driveway was blocked with yellow tape and TV crews crowded the entrance. No one was allowed to enter. I noticed another police car as well. As it drove past, I saw, *police dog*, written on the side window.

Oh thank God. They brought the dogs.

It was good news. Having high hopes he'd find something, I watched every move they made. They charged outside the fence line, but I lost sight of them when they passed the buildings in front.

Several minutes later, they appeared behind Chip's truck and trailer. Intently, I watched the dogs search all around the perimeter, praying they'd find something. With so much focus on the police dogs, I failed to see one of the detectives walk up.

The car door opened again, but this time I jerked around.

"Ms. Ragan, we need to run gun powder tests and take pictures of your hands. This test will help to eliminate you and help us move forward with our immediate investigation. Do we have your consent?"

"Yes, sir," I whispered.

"Okay. I will have one of our processor's here shortly to perform the test."

All I could do was nod my head. The tears had accumulated again and busted through fast. My eyes were swollen now, almost shut, but I couldn't stop the flood. No matter how hard I tried not to cry, I couldn't turn the faucet off. Everything felt like a horrible dream.

The car door opened again and I stepped out.

The officer sprayed both sides of my hands with a wet

substance. It dried quickly. He asked me to hold my hands out, palms down, so I did while he took his pictures.

He then asked for my shoes. I stood there dumbfounded because I didn't understand what he said, not really.

What? He wants my shoes? Why? I can't go barefoot.

The officer repeated the question again, but added, "I only need to take pictures." He must have read my mind.

I removed my muddy sandals and handed them over. He placed them on top of the trunk, took his pictures, and then gave them back. He then reached around me and opened the car door.

"Please get back inside," he said.

But I didn't want to get back inside. I wanted to go home. I wanted to go and be with Chip. I wanted out. Out of the horror flick. I wanted to wake the hell up and know that all of this, every last second of it, was a horrible nightmare.

The officer grabbed my shoulder and I felt a gentle push. Just enough to move me forward. I scooted across the hard seat... and cried.

I'm having a nightmare, I just know I am. But why is this happening? What did I do wrong? Why are you dead, Chip? Why didn't you live?

My cell phone was vibrating again.

It snapped me out of my horrid thoughts. This time it was my mom who was calling. She never called me before 9:00 a.m., *ever*.

I thought about not answering. I knew if I answered she'd be able to tell something was wrong. My finger pushed the button anyway.

"Hello."

"Good morning, sweetie. I know you're busy, Lyn, but I wanted to ask if you can spare a few minutes today to help me with a project."

"Not today, Mom."

She repeated my words, "Not today?"

"No, not today."

How was I going tell her what happened? To say the words out loud, how was I going to do that? I swallowed hard and then forced them out.

"Chip was murdered, Mom. He was shot in the head this morning and he died at the hospital." I thought I was going to vomit. I couldn't believe I'd said those horrible words.

"Oh my God," she screamed.

I told her I was still sitting in a police car and I didn't know when I would be allowed to go home.

"I can't stay on the phone, Mom. I will have to call you later." I had to hang up. The cop had turned down his radio to listen in and was staring at me through the rearview mirror.

I also didn't want her to hear my concern. There was a possibility I may not be able to call her later. Having been confined for hours now, it worried me they might arrest me for Chip's murder. Crazier things have happened.

In this unusual world of sudden horror, I was undeniably trapped. The powerful sadness was overwhelming. I was stuck behind tears that had taken over everything. The wall in front of me was so thick with disbelief; I saw no glimmer of light ahead of me.

Time wouldn't stop either. It played to the beat of a different drum and refused to allow me the common courtesy to catch up.

Time never stopped to reflect … that my life was over.

I needed to get away from the scene of the crime. I had been there long enough and wanted to go home. I desperately needed to get out of the police car.

I looked at the doors but neither had handles on them. I stared up at the cage in front of me, but there was no way out. I was stuck—inside.

I wanted so badly to be with Chip.

I really need to talk to you, my love.

My cell phone vibrated once again. This time it was my sister. I answered as quietly as I could.

"Hey sister."

"Mom called me. Are you all right?" Her voice was calm but filled with a great deal of concern.

"I'm okay," the tears had surfaced again. As much as I tried, there were no other words I could speak.

She was beside herself. I heard her dismay. For whatever reason, my focus seemed blurred. Her voice ran around in my head, but I swore she was standing inside a hollow tunnel somewhere.

I didn't want to talk anyway. I feared if I said anything, I'd be unable to speak it clearly. My thoughts were strong enough—I could hear them—but I knew my voice wouldn't be.

And then it hit me. *Oh my God, it's her birthday.* Today was my sister's birthday, yet, I had nothing inside of me to make her day special.

"Do you want me to call Mom and ask her and Dad to go over to your house and check on it and the kids?" I heard her that time, plain as day.

"Yes, please."

And then I heard the click. I was alone again.

Alone with a speeding train of thoughts. They were swirling around like a massive tornado exploding like little rockets inside my head. I had a massive headache.

The cop had turned the radio up again and every hard beat was literally rattling inside my brain. Thinking became impossible.

"It can't be much longer," I tried to convince myself. "Breathe Lyn, and all of this will be over soon. Then you can go and be with Chip."

Minutes later, I saw movement in the front seat. The cop was putting the car into drive. We were moving forward when I became fixated on the front windshield. There was a circus of people outside. Trucks and vans were lined up everywhere on the side of the road and in the median.

I pressed myself hard against the back seat. I knew the windows were tinted dark, but I couldn't be sure if they'd see me or not. I seriously didn't want to be on the news.

"We're going to head downtown," the officer said. "The detectives who need to talk to you will meet us there."

The sign read, *Homicide Division*. The officer grabbed the door handle, opened it and guided me inside. I knew I was in trouble as I entered.

Why else would I be there?

Somehow, the cloud of despair that hung over me was stronger than worry. My heart wasn't racing with fear. It actually felt empty, yet throbbing in pain.

"Someone will be in to talk with you shortly," the cop said. I didn't jump when the door behind me closed. I stood still, confused and alone.

There was a brown table a few feet in front of me. There were also three orange chairs strategically positioned; one at each corner and one in the middle. It felt like I was in a movie and knew I had to pick a seat.

The room wasn't large. It was about the size of a small dining room. The walls were a pale cream color and looked like office dividers. They reminded me of my own office where I could stick pins in them to hold up letters, or pictures, or memos. There were no windows, no air vents, no lamps, no nothing. It was empty and cold. I was cold.

I sensed something bad coming. It was only a matter of time. I took a seat in the chair located to the left of the table. And then I waited.

Am I going to jail today for something I didn't do?

I was frightened, yes, but the morning events were front and center and stronger than ever. I dropped my head and gazed at my phone resting in my hand. The tears escaped my eyes while I blurrily watched them splash onto my lap.

Every single thought rushed into Chip. I looked for his number, desperately needing to hear his voice. I wanted to beg him, "Please come get me out of here." I needed to ask him, "Where the hell are you?"

I needed Chip to tell me this was all a bad dream.

Yet, I knew if I pushed that button, he wouldn't answer.

And then I heard a noise.

The door opened.

Through watery eyes, I saw a lady walk in. She was an officer dressed in full uniform and her chest was huge; she had to be wearing a bullet proof vest.

Does she think I'm going to shoot her or something?

She had short, dark brown hair. Her legs were small and her body was thin.

"Stand up," she demanded.

Her voice was loud, stern, and cold. I wiped the tears from my face and stood. She raised her hand and motioned me to move closer. "I need to do a body search," she said.

So I did as I was told. I walked closer.

She grabbed my wrists and pulled my arms out to the side and then knelt down.

"Spread your legs," she told me.

I obeyed.

Oh my God, do they seriously think I murdered my fiancé? Why are they doing this to me?

Starting at my ankles, her hands slowly dragged across my legs and inner thighs. When she stood, she searched over my abdomen and then reached behind me. I felt her hands run across my behind and then slowly across my back.

She came around my waist and lifted my breasts, searching under each one. I was braless, still in my pajamas. She moved across my neck and down my arms, then pulled my arms back in front of me. I felt violated.

By the time I realized what had happened, I detected someone pulling my fingers. When I looked, I saw her trying to take my phone from me. I didn't want to release my only link to Chip. I wasn't trying to fight her, but at the same time, I wasn't willing to let her to steal my phone either.

"You have to turn it over," she said, without an ounce of emotion in her voice.

The tears were forming again. This was a battle I wasn't going to win and I knew it. I released my grip and she took the phone. I tried looking into her unemotional eyes, but her gaze darted toward the table.

"Do you have any other possessions with you?"

I had not a shred of strength inside of me to answer. The tears won out and were pouring down my face. I too looked over at the table, but when I did, it appeared so far away.

Is that where I was sitting?

See lady! There's nothing there…

Instead of forming words, I shook my head side-to-side, no. With her rude demeanor and her eyes that screamed *you're guilty*, she turned and walked out the door—with my phone.

She left me there, standing all alone.

I couldn't move. I didn't know what to do. The cold had seeped its way into my bones and I was shaking—and crying. I was screaming inside, stomping my foot at the same time, "Why the hell am I here?"

I forced myself to take a breath. And then I screamed more—"Chip! Where the hell are you? I need you!"

I couldn't move. I was frozen in place.

I pictured myself falling to my knees, curling up into a ball, and screaming as loud as possible. But when my knees wobbled, a strange thought rushed in.

Now is not the time for that, Lyn. Now isn't the time to cry. You'll do that later. This isn't how Chip would want you to react. You have the strength to march through this. Whatever the outcome. It's what he'd want you to do. You know it's what he would do. You're going to be okay. I promise.

Instead of falling to the floor, I turned my eyes toward the table again, and slowly walked over and sat in my chosen seat. Then, I blanked everything out.

I will not think. I will not cry. I will not let these people intimidate me. I didn't do anything wrong. I'm the one who tried to save Chip.

I sat quietly trying to feel nothing. I stared a hole into the floor and didn't move an inch. I knew there was more to come and I was waiting, preparing for the moment. For that exact second when they would accuse me of murdering the love of my life.

Hours ago, when I called for help, it never crossed my mind I'd be accused of hurting him. How naïve was I?

The door opened again.

The same two men I saw hours earlier entered. They placed their notepads on the table and took their respective seats. Detective Finch was the first to speak.

"Can you show me where you've made and received calls this morning?" My phone was in his hands.

I immediately went to the screen, "All Calls", and showed it to the detective, answering all of his questions. I may have spoken a bit unfriendly, but at least I answered them. I was past the point of being irritated with my imprisonment. It was time to let me go home or be charged.

He handed my phone back and asked me to show him the call I received from Chip earlier in the morning. I pointed to the number in the log and then guided him through each call thereafter as I dialed 911, etc.

"Why did he call you so early in the morning?" the second detective asked.

"That's what we do, these are our hours," my eyes lifted to meet his. "We get up early and we go to bed early. Without fail, between four and four-thirty we're on the phone depending on where he has to go. We talk until five-thirty when I have to get ready for work. I call him back once I'm in the car driving between six-thirty and six forty-five. This is what we do, every single day."

They each jotted down notes.

"Do you know of anyone who would want to harm Chip?" Detective Finch asked.

I instantly shook my head. At the same time though, I asked myself, "*Is* there anyone who doesn't like Chip?" And then I thought, yes, maybe one man.

I couldn't imagine he'd dislike Chip so much that he'd want to kill him though. He was also an owner-operator and the only one who caused problems at work. It wasn't possible he disliked Chip to the point that he would kill him. So no, I convinced myself, I don't know of anyone who would want to harm Chip.

"No, I don't know of anyone," I said. But I could hear his name running across my head, *Damone...*

Finch then asked, "Do you know if Chip was involved with drugs of any kind?"

I firmly answered, "No."

"It doesn't matter now if he was. You don't need to protect him anymore."

Offended with his accusation and wanting to protect Chip's name, I asserted, "He wasn't into drugs. He didn't use them. He didn't even drink beer. Chip went this past Friday to have a urinalysis done for the Department of Transportation. We received his results back yesterday; negative for drugs. I swear to you, he didn't use anything."

Just like that, like I had snapped my fingers—it was done. They had nothing else to ask me. A business card was presented and condolences were added.

"If you remember anything, please give us a call." I nodded my head. I knew if I said another word the water behind my eyes would break free.

I was then told the officer who brought me in, would take me home. *Home? I'm going home?*

They both stood, shook my hand, and exited the door. I stared at them until the door closed and then I took a quick glance around the room.

I'm going home.

Chapter Three

SHIPWRECKED

T he nightmare began at 4:45 a.m. and it was now around 11:00 o'clock. The first familiar faces I'd seen all morning were my parents who were standing in my driveway.

The power of the speeding emotions was more than I could bear. As much as I wanted to be by myself to think, I was never so glad to see them standing there.

Nothing, I mean absolutely nothing, felt real. I was on my own, this one Being, breathing amongst a thick, heavy fog sitting in front of me. I swear, nothing was clear.

We walked toward the door and at the same time, my mother was trying to warn me about something. I half-listened. As the door flew open, a wave of shock raced through me. The house was in shambles. There was debris everywhere.

In the middle of the floor sat an enormous pile of rubble. The coffee cup I placed on the counter earlier was lying in front of me, shattered into pieces. My heart sank.

"Oh no! We just bought that china," I whimpered in pain.

When they arrived, my parents were met with a surprise— our large Labrador, Scooby. They had no idea how big he had become. *Only yesterday we took him to the vet and he proudly weighed in at sixty-eight pounds; he was only four months old.* And because Chip and I were bad doggy-parents, we hadn't learned how to teach him right from wrong. Needless to say, when he jumped on them, he scared them.

My mother told me it looked like someone had broken in

and ransacked the house, but it was all Scooby's doing. He had kept himself quite busy while Mommy and Daddy were gone. *Chip's beautiful boy destroyed several DVD's, a dozen CD's, three books, a couple of magazines, and of course the new coffee cup from the counter.*

I needed coffee…badly.

I stepped over the pile on the floor and went to reheat a cup. We then walked outside while I smoked and attempted to share the events of the morning. An hour or so later I escorted them to their car. *They were worried about me, it was written all over their faces.* I wanted them to stay, but I needed them to go. There was no happy medium.

They couldn't help me. No one could help me. Hell, I hadn't the slightest clue what I needed in order to help myself. How could anyone help me?

I walked back inside and stared at Scooby's mess lying on the floor. I cried as I cleaned up the remnants of his disastrous behavior. I saved the book, *The DaVinci Code*, and a couple of DVD covers Chip bought.

"I can't throw anything of yours away, my love. Even if it is broken," I whispered. I knew Chip was dead, but I pretended he wasn't.

What didn't belong to Chip, I threw in the garbage.

I poured myself another cup of coffee and heated it up. Scooby and Angel, our thirteen-year-old Chihuahua, were sitting at my feet, wagging their tails, begging for my attention. I bent down to pet them.

They had no clue Mommy was a shipwrecked mess. They had no idea their daddy was dead. How could they? I felt horrible knowing they would never see him again.

I grabbed Scooby, *Chip's pride and joy*, and pulled him close. I buried my face in his neck… and I cried. He didn't move. Our wild, crazy, jumping, maniac dog, who demanded every second of our focused time—he didn't move. He allowed me to cry.

And then my cell phone rang.

I tried to pull myself together before I answered.

The voice was that of a detective I hadn't met. He was at the lot where Chip's truck and my car still sat. The investigation was still on-going, but would conclude in another hour or two. He told me he'd call when it was time to pick up my car.

At the same time, Chip's mom was calling, too. She asked if I would come over. I said I would after I took a shower. But when I hung up the phone, I couldn't move. I became a zombie, frozen in time.

This is all real, isn't it? Chip was murdered this morning, wasn't he? Everything I thought to be a nightmare earlier is real, isn't it? He's really gone.

I stared into the television a few feet away, looking at my reflection. I looked a mess. I wasn't the same person. And that big 'ole television— it was something Chip insisted we needed to buy.

He couldn't stand the one I had. It was old; a huge Magnavox forty-six inch console. The picture wasn't perfect but it still worked. I didn't watch a lot of TV but he did.

Last summer we headed off to Wal-Mart to buy a new one. He marched straight to the electronics department as I followed behind. We must have checked out a dozen brands, shapes, sizes, and picture qualities too. By the second round, I got bored.

I propped up along an aisle and refused to budge. When he saw me, he laughed. "What are you doing over there? This is your TV we're picking out."

"Sure it is, sweetie. Pick one out so we can go. Please?" I

said, with a big smile planted on my face.

I loved watching him. He had to be so particular, so precise with everything he did. And then, finally, he pointed one out. A forty-one inch Sanyo flat screen.

Thank you Jesus, we can go home now.

We got home, scooted my old monster into the dining room, and then he proceeded to set up the new one. By the time I took the kids out to potty and made us something to drink, he had the VCR and the stereo all hooked up to the new TV and ready to play.

I stood in the doorway of the kitchen and watched him as he planted himself on the sofa. He then threw his feet up on the coffee table, got comfortable, turned the TV on, and looked very proud of himself. After flipping through a bunch of channels he finally acknowledged me. We both laughed.

He had a new TV to watch here at his second home—Chip was happy. I had to admit, the picture quality was amazing.

Back and forth I rocked.

Clasping my face.

With every gut wrenching breath I took, I couldn't stop crying. That voice I heard earlier—the time would come later to cry—this must be it, the time to cry.

I felt Scooby brush up against my leg and I sensed Angel sitting on the couch beside me. Neither nagged me or touched me. They sat quietly and allowed me to go through the torment that had taken over everything. I couldn't see them. I couldn't see anything. My tears were raining too hard…

Awhile later, I tried to wipe them from my face and stare up at the fireplace mantle. The violent convulsions were attacking my body, but my focus was in one spot—a picture of Chip in his Scottish kilt.

My memory took me back in time to the day he handed me that picture. It was last year in March, a bright sunny Sunday morning.

We headed out for breakfast like we normally did, when he shared something out of character.

"Oh," he said, "I printed you a picture of me in my kilt. You can put it on top of your fireplace and then you'll have me to look at whenever I'm not there." He then patted my leg twice.

I questioned his comment silently, "Is he nuts?" But he busted into laughter instantly and I joined him. I couldn't help but wonder if he was serious though.

After breakfast we headed back to his house to say "Hi" to his mom. Once inside, Chip disappeared into his computer room. I sat chatting with his mother, enjoying our conversation. A few minutes later he walked around the corner and headed toward me, holding something in his hand.

There it was. A photo of him in his Scottish attire. I tried not to laugh, but I couldn't help it.

"You were serious, weren't you?" I said with a snort.

"Of course I was."

"All righty then," I giggled, "I'll buy a frame for it and put it right on top of the fireplace. Just like you said. How's that sound?"

I knew he had to be laughing inside too. But he didn't show it. Instead, he was calm, smiling big.

"Sounds good to me," he said, with no real emotion.

A day later I went to CVS Pharmacy to see if they had any decent looking frames. I found one I fell in love with. Antiquity quality, but sophisticated, as well.

I bought it, took it home and immediately placed his photo inside. I did as I promised—I put his picture on top of the mantle.

I didn't tell him about the frame. The following day he came over and let himself in. I was in another room working when I heard his laughter from inside the living room. I hurried in and saw him standing at the fireplace, hands in his pockets, staring at his picture.

He turned to face me and when he did, I noticed something different—his smile. It was one I hadn't seen before. His expression was much more gentle and soft. That's when I knew something between us changed. He was as proud to be a part of my life as I was to be a part of his.

I smiled back, looked up at his picture and said, "You look good up there, sweetie pie."

Back in the here and now, the kids started barking.

Once again they distracted me, but that was a good thing. I was oh so close to sinking into a complete and reckless depression. The last place I needed to be was on memory lane.

I got up and walked outside. I took my coffee and sipped it while we sat under the sun.

The air was cool.

The sky was beautiful and the brightest of blue. It was the first time I noticed the sky that day. The night before it had stormed but you'd never know it now. Funny how quickly things change.

I went over and over, the events of the entire morning. I tried to remember our conversation before he stepped out of the truck, but I had forgotten it.

I tried to think of all the things I could have done differently, too. What if I would have stayed by the road to wait for the rescue and not by Chip—would those minutes have made a difference? Would they have saved his life?

Why didn't I insist he come home instead of going to work? He wouldn't be dead—why didn't I? Why didn't I sense more urgency when he said those words, *oh shit?* I could have been there sooner.

Minutes lost. Minutes that could have saved him. Why didn't I save him?

Out of nowhere, Scooby scratched the door.

I had no sense of time and no clue how much had passed. The detective would be calling soon, so I decided to go in and take a quick shower.

Thinking was doing me more harm than good. Shutting off my thoughts was key. The next few hours were going to be tough and self-loathing wasn't going to help.

Besides… none of it was real. I was amid a nightmare. One I couldn't control. As soon as I woke up, everything would go back to normal.

"That's right, Lyn, it's just a dream."

This sort of thing doesn't happen in real life.

Chapter Four

INFINITI

The call from the detective came while I was showering. I threw on my clothes and called Chip's mom. I informed her it was time to pick up the vehicles and I'd be over shortly to get her. The only car I had to drive was the new one Chip and I had bought last week.

We purchased our first car together last Monday, an Infiniti M45. Sitting inside of it and turning the key, it made me think of our weekend together.

We drove out to the beach to pick up my engagement ring; it had to be resized. The ring was gorgeous. I told Chip a thousand times how much I loved it. He loved me so much; it was sometimes too hard to believe.

On our way home, we had a rather in depth conversation. One that made me feel a twinge of guilt for being a real penny pincher. Through and through, I was, and I knew it.

Going hungry when I was younger and married to a man who wouldn't get a job, I made a promise to myself—to never depend on another man to feed me. I kept that promise. I made a career for myself and didn't need anyone to take care of me.

I was extremely fragile when it came to spending money unnecessarily. Chip on the other hand, spent it like it grew on trees. I had to budget money for him just to blow.

Chip wants us to buy a new car, so that's what we're going to do. It's time to stop watching every dime we spend.

I searched online and kept it a secret.

I remembered a conversation he and my sister had the year before when they talked about Infiniti's, but I couldn't remember the model nor could I ask him about it. I found several M25s but I didn't like the body style. Only one car kept my interest. It was an M45 with low mileage and a decent price. I printed out the information.

I'll surprise him when I get home.

We got so caught up in chit chatting, I almost forgot the surprise. As soon as I gave it to him though, he was too interested in it for my liking. I should've seen the writing on the wall when he grabbed my hand and dragged me to the computer room to pull it up online.

He sat me on his lap and wrapped his arm around my waist so I couldn't get away. We searched other cars, but in the end we both agreed that we liked the M45 the best.

I guess I figured we'd talk about it, dream a little bit about it, and then search more. Possibly go look at one or two the coming weekend. That's what we did together; we searched. We were getting pretty good at it, too.

"Well, let's go check it out," Chip said. I was stunned.

"Right now? It's 4:30 in the afternoon. The traffic will be horrible. Not to mention we go to bed early."

I knew he sensed my apprehension.

"What are you afraid of? Do you think we might like it and buy it today?"

Yes, that's exactly what I was afraid of. He was reading my mind and I didn't like that. I knew Chip. When he liked something, especially if we didn't already have it, consider it bought.

But I vowed earlier I wanted us to be happy in whatever we did. I needed to keep my promise. My penny pinching days had to end. So I lied, "Of course not."

Yet I knew—*I knew*—if that car was sweet, we'd be driving her home tomorrow. The look of excitement on his face was priceless. I had no choice. I had to give in.

"All right, let's go." I didn't need to say another word. Within minutes we were flying out the door.

Chip parked us along the service road, right outside the car lot. My phone rang before he turned the truck off, so I answered it as he stepped out. I finished my call and hopped down, but he was nowhere in sight; he had left me there. When I looked further down the road, I saw him trotting back.

Instantly, I noticed his smile. It was huge. And though I couldn't detect his eyes hidden behind his dark reflective sunglasses, I imagined they were bright too.

"You are going to love this car!" he shouted.

"You went and looked at it without me?" I said.

I was surprised by his behavior but smitten at the same time. He was so cute.

"I couldn't help myself. You are going to fall in love with this car, sweetie." A little boy had emerged.

Chip grabbed me up and hugged me tightly—right in the middle of the street. His excitement was powerful. He gave me a big kiss, caressed my hand, and then pulled me to walk... quickly.

"I still can't believe you went without me." I spanked him.

He pointed to the car, and yes, it was beautiful. It wasn't brand new, it had a scratch here and there, but compared to our present rides, she was gorgeous.

Chip opened the passenger door and I slid in. He jogged around the front and hopped in the driver's seat. We marveled at the gadgets, checked out the many compartments, and soaked up her new car smell.

"The sales lady will bring the key in a minute. I've already given her my license," he said, with pure joy.

Wow, he works fast.

In that moment it didn't matter, it felt good. The key was presented and off we went. The traffic was a little heavy on Blanding Boulevard, but I insisted he give her a little boost to see what she could do. She was equipped with a V8 for heaven's sake; we both knew she had power.

I was sucked straight back into the seat when he floored her. Our laughter filled the car. We were having a great time.

And then he pulled over to the side of the road.

"What are you doing?" I asked.

"I want you to drive and we should turn around to go back."

"No, sweetie pie, we don't have to go back yet. That's why they call this a test drive. We won't learn anything about her in a five minute ride. Keep going."

"Are you sure?" he asked.

"Absolutely!"

Chip drove us close to the intersection of 103rd Street, a few miles from the dealership. He then made a U-turn and pulled over to an empty side street, insistent that I drive now.

So I scooted over into the driver's seat, waited for him to get comfortable, put her into drive, checked both ways, and slowly moved out onto the road. Before I pushed the pedal, I looked over at him one last time.

"Are you ready?" I asked.

"For what?" he replied.

But I didn't answer. I just smiled big, looked to make sure no other cars appeared, and stomped on the gas pedal.

Holy smoke, this car is fast.

I was whooping and hollering and laughing, having a grand time. I saw his hands fly out and grab the dashboard; he was holding on tight. I was cracking up, laughing my butt off when

I heard my name mixed in with a shriek of words.

"Lynnie! Slow your ass down! You're going to wreck us and we don't own her yet."

I couldn't help it—that made me laugh even more. I slowed her down. But only because I didn't want to make him nervous. He may not let me drive, ever again.

"You're a crazy woman!" he howled.

Crazy or not, oh my gosh, that was fun.

I found a place to pull over and we changed places again. My calm, cool, and collected man drove us back to the dealership. When he put her in park and turned her off, he had the most serious look on his face.

"We have to buy her. She's perfect," he said.

"Are you serious?" I was a bit startled. I already knew the answer before he even said it. Chip wanted that car.

For months we had discussions pertaining to our credit scores and mortgage rates, etc. His score was much better than mine and it was our security blanket for getting into a new home. To have a new purchase added to his credit history would cause his score to drop dramatically and he knew it. This was his bargaining chip and he used it to the hilt.

"Absolutely, I'm serious," he said, while he gently caressed the steering wheel. Next came the defining moment I knew she was about to be ours.

"Darlin, if you don't, I will. And you know what will happen then. Right?"

All I could do was laugh, out loud. I didn't take his comment as bribery per se, although that's exactly what he was doing. Rather, I took it as a clue to how serious he wanted us to have such a sweet ride.

After we both stopped laughing, I stared into his eyes. "Okay. Let's go see how much we can bargain with these people."

And that's what we did. We walked inside and bargained for thirty plus minutes while sipping coffee. They reduced the price three thousand dollars.

I signed the papers to agree to pay for it the next day upon approval from my bank. And then we left. On our ride home we discussed our payment options. He wanted to put money down to reduce the financing and lower the payments. I called the bank and got approved. We agreed he'd pay the car payment and I would take care of the insurance. We both got what we wanted... a new car... and neither had to endure the entire financial burden.

All of the excitement made us a tad hungry so we stopped at one of our favorite seafood spots to grab a bite to eat. The next day, we hurried to the dealership to pay for, and bring our new baby home. They had her all cleaned up; she shined like nobody's business, like the sun sitting over the ocean.

After being handed the key, he tried to give it to me but I wouldn't have it. I couldn't take it away from him—the first drive of a new car.

"I'll drive the Acura, sweetie. You drive the Infiniti."

"But why?" he asked.

"Because I want you to. Stay close in case something happens though."

I watched his movements in the car in the rearview mirror, as much as I could. He had a time getting the seat comfortable for his long legs. I saw him reach over to the radio display; he looked so happy.

Chip was proud. He was like a child in a candy factory. On January 15, 2008, I was happy for him, and for us. Our future was being formed. We were having fun.

I snapped back.

Into reality again. There I was, driving slowly to his house. Getting it stuck in my head—*he's dead*—that wasn't coming easy. The tears just kept pouring.

I felt like a ghost somehow, floating around with no real destination. I was lost. Lost as lost could be. My hands were the only steering component to my body. The rest of me... on auto-pilot. Somehow, I kept moving.

After picking up his mom, I drove toward the lot. That place was dead to me. I didn't want to go back there. I drove extra slow and took the longest route possible.

We discussed all the possibilities—who murdered Chip?

"I asked Chip to show me who did this to him and he showed me Damone. It's him, I know it's him," Char said.

I'd always known she had a sixth sense. But hearing her say Chip "showed her" who killed him? I didn't know where to file that. She was convinced Damone did it.

She had accompanied Chip at work a couple of times last year—she knew who Damone was. She watched him once from a distance and even told Chip he needed to watch his back around him. She'd felt that uneasy around Damone.

I didn't want to believe Chip and I worked with a killer, so I tried to convince myself it still didn't fit.

"Why would he kill Chip?" I asked.

"Why wouldn't he? He's obviously jealous of him, envious of Chip's personality because he doesn't have one. He did this, Lyn. I know he did."

"I don't know. It doesn't make any sense."

"It makes perfect sense," she insisted.

I suddenly remembered my own thoughts earlier that morning. His name was the only one I came up with when asked if I knew anyone who would want to harm Chip. I knew it was him.

We both knew it. Damone killed Chip. Yet, there wasn't a single thing we could do. We had to wait and see where the investigation led. Even though Damone's jealousy was shared with the police, it wasn't evidence that he murdered Chip.

We drove into the entrance of the big empty lot.

Everything sat exactly the way I left it. Except now there was no spirit or purpose. There was no life. It all died—right along with Chip. I stood there, alone in my vacant mind, staring at his big truck.

There were a couple of times I brought myself back to earth. I got lost and thought I was waiting for him. It felt like he was right there. Like he was only seconds behind me. I even looked back me a few times searching for him. I could have sworn he was walking up.

And then I gravitated to the spot where we spent our last minutes together—where he laid bleeding to death. I stared at the ground that was now disturbed, his blood mixed in with the mound of mud.

I could see his body still lying there.

The vision was clear—so clear I could reach out and touch him. The magnitude of the day, of his death… it wasn't sinking in.

He couldn't be dead.

Chapter Five

THIS DAY NEVER ENDS

O nce I was home, car in tow, I was alone to dive into my sorrow. I had asked my sister to wait until the following day to come up. She was obviously worried about me.

"I won't be myself. I'm sure I'll be with Char and the rest of Chip's family. I'll be okay," I assured her.

I knew she didn't want me to be alone, and I truly believed I'd be with family. But I was in for a big surprise. A few minutes after I hung up with her, I learned I'd indeed be alone. Chip's family was gathering together—but I wasn't invited.

I seriously didn't see that coming.

It was okay, though. It didn't surprise me. Or shock me even. As a matter of fact, it put me in my place rather quickly. This was the story of my life—to deal with life's blows—alone. It certainly wasn't the first time I felt let down and I was positive it wouldn't be the last.

My afternoon, and the rest of the day, was going to be painfully tormenting. I knew that. My mind was full, my heart was empty, my everything was completely gone. I had no clue what I was supposed to do, how I was supposed to feel, or how I was supposed to accept Chip's death.

I cried out, "How do I feel this Chip? I can't believe you aren't here. I can't believe any of this is true."

I collapsed to the floor and screamed in pain.

It was horrible—the physical agony I felt—yet I hadn't lost any part of my physical body. It was a God-awful hurt, and it was being distributed throughout every part of me. My heart was active; I could feel it pounding inside my chest. It had feelings and emotions but today—today it was dying. Instead of pumping blood through my circulatory system, it was forcing a class of torture I'd never experienced before.

I was numb. I felt nothing. But I felt everything. I felt—so freaking lost. I sat on the sofa, threw my face into my hands, and travelled a lonely road to a torturous hell. I never imagined one person could release such a flood of tears.

They were unending. They flowed effortlessly. In grave detail, they described everything I was experiencing.

Out of nowhere, the doorbell rang, pulling me back into reality. The kids barked crazily, running wild between the front door and the front window. Once again, my hellish torment was put on hold.

I grabbed my sunglasses and went to see who it was.

There were three men standing on the front porch. Two of them I recognized as the detectives I interacted with earlier. The other was a tall, slim black man whom I'd seen on television a few hours ago. I had watched him give details about Chip's murder; he was asking the public for help in finding the attacker.

I walked outside.

Detective Finch asked, "Can you tell me what you know of a man named Damone?" I was shocked to hear him say that name.

"Char and I spoke of him this morning. She believes he's responsible. I don't know anything about him from a personal standpoint, but at work we've learned he's a jealous and nosy man. He doesn't know how to mind his own business."

I stopped and looked at him closely.

"What reason would he have to murder Chip?" I asked.

The tall detective interjected, "People will kill anyone, even over a French fry."

He was right. How true was that? Every single day people are killed for no reason. His words grabbed my attention and I stood there, hooked. But then Finch's voice raced in, disturbing my zoned out thoughts.

How long was I standing there in silence?

"Did the two of you know anyone, or associate with anyone, who drives a yellow car?"

I thought for a moment, running rapidly through my mind of the people we knew. But I couldn't think of anyone.

"No, we kept to ourselves. We don't have too many friends here like we do down south." But then it occurred to me. "Oh my, God, yes! Damone drives a yellow car."

My mind flew into overdrive.

What do they know? Why are they asking about that car?

But I had no time to gather answers. Detective Finch was asking more questions.

"Do you know what kind of car it is?"

"Yes, it's a smaller car, two doors."

"Do you remember if it's a Honda or a...?"

"I think it's a Honda."

"Do you remember any markings or stripes?"

"There are black stripes on the side of the car. The black stripes go all across the car."

"Can you remember if it has a spoiler or not?"

"I believe so, yes."

Curiosity was racing through my veins. They were all jotting down notes and I was off in space somewhere. Right then, without question, I knew for certain Damone murdered Chip. But the silence ended as fast it landed.

"Do you know where he lives?"

"I don't have his address with me, but I can get it for you in the morning from work."

"That will be fine," he said.

"May I ask why you're questioning me about this car?"

"There was a witness who called in and described a car leaving the scene this morning around the same time that Chip was murdered."

"So you think this is the person who murdered Chip?"

"We have reason to believe so, yes."

His voice lingered there for a long time. He then asked me to give him a call as soon as I could supply him the address and I told him I would. The three of them got in their car and drove away.

"It's him," I admitted out loud. "I thought of him this morning. Char's convinced it's him. And now there's a witness who can identify his car. They know who killed Chip!"

That car. There are those who would compare that car to a *rice burner*. The exhaust system had a distinctive sound and when you hear one of these cars going down the road, the noise from it sounds *exactly* like a loud lawnmower engine.

It was gradually making a bit more sense. That terrible loud sound I heard in the phone—that was why. That car drove right up to Chip's head. Yes! That was it.

It took several years to learn this wasn't true. The car did not drive up to Chip's head and it wasn't the sound I heard; the lawnmower sound, that is. The sound I heard was the sound of the bullets traveling through Chip's head. His Bluetooth picked up the vibration of the bullets as they entered and exited.

Back inside the house, I tried to make sense of the events that were slowly unfolding.

"I should have said his name this morning—I didn't want to believe it was him. It's inconceivable the evil that runs through that wicked man. Why do I need to wait until tomorrow? I can call work now."

So I did.

I wrote the address on the back of Detective Finch's card. I turned the card over, called the number listed, and left a message supplying him with Damone's address, repeating it twice.

I hung the phone up, placed it on the kitchen counter, and dizzily walked into the living room. My eyes traveled upward, to Chip's picture resting on top of the mantle. I gazed at him as the tears streamed over my face again. It was sinking in.

"I'm not dreaming, am I? This is real, isn't it?"

Chip was gone. Forever.

How could I live without him?

As my tear-filled eyes stared deeply into his, it hit me—he was never going to kiss me again. He was never going to wrap his big strong arms around me, his beautiful blue eyes would never gaze into mine—his sweet voice was never again, going to dance in my ear.

How was I going to live without ever seeing his gorgeous smile? Or sleep beside him? I seriously didn't know what to do.

The raging sadness inside devoured me. The physical point of sobbing was falling into the past. A horrible and constant cry had now consumed me.

I sat there alone, and cried—uncontrollably.

Hours later, Scooby stuck his nose on my lap.

The kids were begging to go outside; they needed to potty. I opened the door and suddenly became aware that I needed to make an attempt at sleep. I had to work the following day.

Even though we kept our relationship away from work, I thought it best to protect our secret, still. But with my present spirit, sleep wasn't going to be easy.

I fed the kids, tried to eat a piece of toast, put Visine drops in my eyes, brushed my teeth, and hopped into bed. I pulled the covers over my head and tasted the tears as they slid across my lips.

My phone rang.

It was seven-thirty at night and the last thing I wanted was to talk. The number on the phone was unknown, but so were a dozen others today, all from police officers and detectives. In case it was another, I answered. It was Detective Finch.

I was surprised to hear his voice. I was even more surprised when he told me he and his partner were sitting in front of Damone's house.

He said, "The car in question, that matches the description from the witness given this morning, is sitting here in front of us. I need to ask you a couple more questions."

"Okay." I was willing to do anything to help Chip.

The immediate excitement, for lack of a better word, at the possibility of the shooter being caught on the same day consumed my every thought. I was allowed, however, to share a little more about Chip.

"Chip considered Damone his friend," I told him. "He would always help him strap down his loads. Only two months ago, Chip purchased two bars to tighten down his straps and actually gave one of them to Damone. Anytime I saw the two of them in the yard at the same time, Chip was always conversing with him, laughing and joking around."

That was what confused me so much. Chip never had anything bad to say about Damone. Granted, he didn't spend much time around him, but he always defended the type of person he was. I guess I assumed the feeling was mutual.

The one time Damone came up in a conversation, Chip said, verbatim, "He's all right baby doll. He's a good guy. He doesn't know how to communicate, that's all."

I never saw what he saw.

The moment I met Damone, his eyes clearly stated he was no good. That eerie feeling, like he was evil, swept over me. I was always uncomfortable around him. He never had to do anything or even say anything—being in the same room was enough to give me the creeps. I always had that uncontrollable push to exit the room whenever he was near.

I wasn't the only one that felt it either. The other girls in the office did as well. It was in his eyes. Bad, bad, wicked eyes.

Having said that, it was mandatory I kept my personal opinion to myself. Personality conflicts aside, my responsibility was to focus on moving the product to the stores as required. I rarely spoke to the contractors and/or the owner operators. Our yard manager was responsible for everything they did.

"Is he not home?" I asked Detective Finch.

"No, he's not home. We'll stay here and wait for him though. I believe we have the information we need. I'll be in contact with you soon. Thank you for your help."

I visualized them sitting outside of Damone's house. Having seen the car at work, it was easy to picture them in front of it. It was a two-door Honda.

A bright bumblebee yellow, coated the car. The hood was flat black and each side of the car had slanted black striping. A picture of a skull and crossbones was on the driver-side and passenger-side windows. It was an unmistakable car.

What will they say to him? Will they arrest him? Tonight?

I laid in bed for hours and wondered.

That evil, evil man planned every step of murdering Chip. He stalked him, preyed upon him, and then snuck up on Chip, in the dark, and shot him in the head. What a coward, yet, conniving enough to hide in wait.

He wanted to kill Chip. And he did what he set out to do.

Will Chip's death be avenged tonight? God I hope so!

Chapter Six

SAYING GOODBYE

I t felt like a dagger was thrust in my body inflicting a pain so horrible I couldn't breathe. I swore a hole existed inside somewhere, so deep that it was sucking up every ounce of energy I had.

I wanted badly to pull my chest wide open and scream as loud as I could, "Take me now. Please don't let me lie here and suffer!"

But all I could do was walk in a daze of complete denial. My mind knew and understood it completely—Chip was dead. But my heart... my heart refused to accept any part of that truth.

The war had begun.

Arrangements were made. The announcement went out to family members and friends. I heard the plans, and then quickly dismissed them. I walked in a mist of secrecy believing that Chip wasn't dead.

One minute I'd convinced myself his death wasn't real, and that I was living inside a hellish nightmare desperately waiting to be pinched awake. Everything around me certainly appeared to be tangible, but I knew better. I knew he wasn't gone.

And then, in the next minute, I could see it with my own eyes—he had vanished. I hadn't spoken with him in days. The anguish of seeing it and acknowledging it, followed with the rushing river of tears—his death had all but consumed me.

All I wanted to do was crawl into our bed, go to sleep, and

never wake again. I wanted to be with Chip and nothing else mattered. Without him, my life was gone; it was over. The moment I found him lying flat on his back, my life, too, ended.

But my sister had a way of interfering with my wants—she guided me forward. The only time I was allowed out of her sight, was at bedtime.

Chip's funeral service was set for Monday, January 28th. However, on Sunday, we were allowed to visit Chip before his body was cremated. It would be the first time I'd see him since he died.

I wanted a different picture of Chip rather than the one I was left with. The one where all I saw was him fighting for his life while his head lay in a massive puddle of his own blood.

I reasoned with myself that seeing him in a much different setting, lying peacefully, would help ease the pain that was literally ripping me apart.

I was right. But I was also very wrong.

Before reaching the door that led to Chip, I had to first walk a long, empty hallway adorned with red carpet and extravagant paintings.

I stood outside the golden door and took a deep breath before forcing my feet to move forward. Not sure of what I might see, I slowly shuffled into a dark, cold room.

The love of my life ... lying in a damn wooden box.

He looked peaceful enough. Like he was sleeping restfully. But he didn't look like Chip. In fact, he looked like someone else entirely. I was shocked.

Chip was lying in a casket made of wood that wasn't as big as he was. His shoulders were the widest part of his body. But now? If I didn't know better, I would swear someone stood on top of him, jumped up and down a few times, and crammed him in nice and tight. That wasn't the same man. Not the one who was full of life only a couple of days ago.

And his face—oh, his poor face.

Both of his eyes were black and blue. The woman who escorted us in said they were bruised because of the bullet that entered at the right side of his head—about an inch from his ear—and then exited through the back.

Little red spots, speckling, covered his eyes. They covered his cheeks, all around his nose, and near his mouth and chin. Before today, I had no idea what gunpowder burns looked like.

In order to receive such red marks, Chip was shot at close range. The gun was fired at his head literally within two feet.

The right-side of the tip of his nose was missing. Makeup was used to disguise the missing flesh. *At the time, we had no idea the first shot fired, was through Chip's nose.* Being the little detectives his mom and I professed to be, we thought either the perpetrator knocked him out with a tool bar, or he fired a shot and Chip tried to duck, causing the flesh from his nose to be ripped away.

Either scenario would have caused him to fall straight back, giving the shooter access to fire a single bullet into his head. *It took four long years to learn there were actually two bullet wounds in Chip's head.* We didn't know if there was more than one perpetrator and quite possibly two guns. What we did know—the killer was still free.

Chip's hair was shaven and a white towel had been placed across his head. I supposed the funeral home did that so we wouldn't see the bullet holes behind his ear. I didn't look.

I grabbed his hand though. It was freezing cold, but I clung to him for dear life. I knew he couldn't hear me, so I pretended he could as I spoke to him silently.

I told him how sorry I was. I told him how much I loved

him. How much I missed him. I stared at his closed eyes and wished... hard... for them to open.

I didn't want to release him. Even if he didn't look like Chip, it was still him. And I knew today was it. These were our last physical moments together.

It would be mere minutes before he became ashes.

The room was quite small.

His casket was only a few feet from the entrance, located to the right. A deep red, velvet sofa was positioned against the opposite wall. There were two small end tables, each holding a small dimly lit lamp that provided the only light in the room. A dark coffee table sat directly in front of the sofa, cleared of any contents.

The room was freezing cold, gloomy and dreary.

As the moments passed and family arrived, I sat on the red sofa in silence, watching. And then the darndest feeling crept over me. I could see everything and everyone around me, but the sense was like—well, it was like none of it was real.

I wasn't dizzy or foggy. It felt more like—like what I was seeing in front of me was a figment of my imagination. I swore I heard someone whisper, "It's just an illusion."

The whisper scared me. I grabbed my wrist and searched for my pulse. It was vital I make sure I wasn't dreaming.

"This is crazy!" I told myself.

Suddenly, someone screamed—very loud.

"Chip isn't dead! No! He's not dead."

No one turned around—I was the only one who heard the cry. It must have originated from somewhere inside my head. My heartbeat sped up quickly, but I couldn't move. I sat in utter shock. And then the door creaked open.

It was the lady from the funeral home telling us our time

was almost over. The voice ultimately disappeared because my thoughts rushed back to Chip. I didn't want to leave him. He was dead, lying inside a wooden box, but at least he was there. I jumped up and ran to his side.

"Let's all write a note to Chip and place it with him so he'll have them forever," his mom said. So we did.

We scrambled around to find paper and pen. I placed my note in his right hand and then, one-by-one, I watched everyone else place theirs. I was the last to walk out and stopped in the hall to watch the door close.

"Together forever, my wonderful Chippey. For the rest of my life, I will miss you. I promise, you will live in my heart forever."

Our last goodbye transpired the next day.

Chip's service was lovely. The house was full to capacity and still there were people standing along the back walls, in the hallway, and out the front doors. Many came to pay their last respects to a man who had touched their lives in so many ways.

He was only forty-one years old. Too young to die. Especially that way.

Chip was honored with the most beautiful sound of bagpipes playing his favorites, *Amazing Grace* and *Danny Boy*. And then, the Navy saluted him with their Twenty-One-Gun Salute. It truly was a wonderful ceremony.

After the reception ended, we headed home. I was glad to get away from the constant sound of chatter. It was too much. It was a hard and confusing day for me. I had no idea how to say goodbye to someone I loved more than life itself.

He was perfectly fine a few days ago. There wasn't anything wrong with him. As a matter of fact, he was physically healthy. Seriously. How do you say goodbye to someone who loved to live?

Nothing made sense.

I couldn't say goodbye.

Earlier in the week, I was told no bullets were recovered. I couldn't imagine why. There had to be something they didn't see or something they missed. So on my way home, I decided to drive by the empty and desolate lot and take a look.

That evil maniac needed to get to his resting place—in prison—and I wanted to help with that. But after searching all around Chip's truck and trailer, there was nothing to be found.

There was something new, however. Sticks. There were sticks scattered about with yellow paint. I noticed a few holes in the ground around the trailer, too. Each one had a hard, yellow substance mixed in with the dirt.

Still pretending Chip was alive, I said it out loud.

"They have his foot prints, darlin."

I walked around for an hour more, but found nothing else. It was also time to say my farewells to my sister since she was going back to Fort Lauderdale. So I headed home.

In a weird way, I had become dependent upon her. She was my guide and my rock, while I trampled through this thing called, *Chip's death.*

I truly feared being left alone.

Yet, I also knew it was time for reality to hit, head on. Either I was going to sink, or I was going to swim. There wasn't an in between—there was no choice. Damone made sure *no one* had a choice about anything.

He stripped my future husband away. And Chip—he just disappeared. Vanished. Into thin air. Taken, his life wiped out.

God, I missed him madly...

I didn't want to be alone.

After my sister left, I walked back inside to a quiet house. I changed out of my funeral clothes and slipped into one of

Chip's long sleeved shirts. It was my way of staying close to him. I fed the kids and then took them outside to run around.

I sat outside for hours. My mind raced wildly, flying into an empty place of blankness. I zombie'd out while staring a hole into space somewhere. And then I felt them.

The mountain of salty tears ready to break the dam.

They welcomed me home. Their sudden descent told me I had held them in for far too long and that being strong wasn't a smart idea. If Chip could still see me, I wanted to make him proud and not shed the tears in front of everyone today.

Through my foggy and rainy eyes I stared up into the blue sky above. With all my might, I mustered the energy to shout. If Chip was up there, out there somewhere, I needed him to know how I felt.

"I love you with every ounce of my Being, Chip Oney. I am *so* sorry this happened to you. If I could change anything my love, I would rather it be me and not you. I am so very, very sorry!"

EVIL EYES

M y eyes were swollen and burned badly. Visine wasn't fixing them. There wasn't anything that could disguise my grief-stricken heart. Before bed though, I added a few more drops hoping to reduce the swelling.

The day had been a long one filled with confusion. I put the kids up for the night and forced myself to crawl into bed. I had to work the next day and needed sleep. It should come easy. It had been days since I rested and truth be known, I was mentally exhausted.

I laid my head down and grabbed Chip's pillow. I wrapped my arms around it and cradled it tightly. Using it to smother my face, I cried until I couldn't think anymore. Somehow, sleep took over my weary mind and body. I was out.

"When did I wake up? Whoa! I don't remember waking up."

I couldn't remember getting out of bed either. I rubbed my eyes to wipe the sleepy away while I walked through the living room. I was heading outside. I opened the back door and took one step down. I looked out into the yard searching for the kids, but I didn't see them anywhere.

"Why have I walked outside without the kids?"

I never went outside without them. I couldn't figure it out— why I was alone.

"Holy crap! Who's that? Am I seeing what I think I'm seeing?"

I saw a distant figure walking through the rear fence. He was approaching my back yard. I bent down to hide but also to see through the branches too. I wanted to make sure I could see him more clearly.

"Yes, there he is."

It was a man... and he literally walked, or was he floating?, right through my chain link fence.

"How'd he do that?" I voiced out loud.

My curiosity skyrocketed. I watched his every move as he sauntered toward the tree in the middle of the yard. I saw where he was headed and knew he'd wind up in my neighbor's front lawn. As he got closer though, I panicked.

"What if he sees me? I should run in and get my gun," I told myself. I stood up and turned to walk inside.

"No. That'll take too long. He might follow me. God knows I don't want that. He might hurt the kids."

I turned back and walked to the edge of the steps. I eyed him again, watching him, hard. The man was still marching forward.

"Okay. He's not going to bother me. I'll be fine," I said.

I could now see he was covered in black clothing. His hands were tucked inside his pants pockets causing him to have a peculiar stance. He was also hunched over a little bit.

The man wore a black sweat shirt with a big hoody. I noted the hoody was somewhat pointed at the tip. Everything on him was black. Everything.

"Damn he feels wicked. He's up to something bad."

But he hadn't looked my way—not once. And that was good. To get a better view, I took two steps down the stairs. Unexpectedly... he turned his head and stared at me.

My heart flopped. He was walking toward me. His steps were getting bigger and bigger, and he was getting closer and closer.

"Who the hell are you?" I screamed out.

I was scared. Scared to death. But at the same time, I knew I couldn't back down. I had to protect the kids. I knew I wasn't going to run away. I felt a new field of strength inside, protecting me.

The closer he got, the easier it was to detect the features of his face. He was a black man. And his eyes... he had the brightest, greenest, and wickedest cat-looking eyes I'd ever seen. I felt evil like I'd never felt before as it slammed hard into my chest.

The fear was knocking at my stubbornness to shield myself. My feet were shaking badly. I was scared. So scared, I started talking to myself again.

"It's too late, Lyn, to turn and run into the house. You're here now. And obviously not going anywhere. Why am I here?"

I stood my ground, afraid to move. I blinked. In a flash, he was there, right in front of me. The man reached out with both of his hands and grabbed the side railings.

Slowly, God-awfully slow, he crawled forward like a cat stalking its prey. He was so close; his wicked eyes were right in front of mine. I felt the hot air from his breath brush my chin.

In a deep, creepy, whispering tone, he said...

"W . h . e . r . e . ' . s y . o . u . r m a . m . a ?"

I screamed at the top of my lungs. The wicked man had scared the hell out of me. My body jerked hard and my head fell back.

Everything went dark and at the same time, I was being lifted—up. My upper body was rising up, into a sitting position. I had no control of anything except my voice. I was screaming, loudly...

...screaming at the top of my lungs. I never howled so loud

in all my life. And then it clicked. I wasn't outside.

I was sitting straight up, in bed—eyes tightly closed.

Slowly, I opened them.

My body was drenched in sweat.

"What just happened?" I screeched out. "What the hell was that?" It hadn't registered yet—it was a dream.

"Was he real?" I took a breath, "Holy crap he was real!"

I leaped out of bed, grabbed my gun, unlocked the bedroom latch, and tiptoed through the house. Slowly, I opened the back door and peeked outside. There was no one there.

I proceeded to take one step down.

Striking a pose like one of the women in, *Charlie's Angels,* I stood firm, pointing the gun. With squinted eyes, I searched hard into the dark, looking for the wicked green-eyed man.

But he wasn't there.

I released the pose and dropped the gun to my side.

"Shit! That felt real!" I said under my breath.

Chapter Eight

IT'S JUST A DREAM

To fear someone inside of a dream seemed irrational. I knew the only thing to fear was fear itself. But truth be known, that dream was as real as being wide awake. I had never experienced anything like it before.

I was never one to give *sleeping dreams* a second thought; they were just dreams. With this one though, I wasted no time checking on both of our mothers—just in case. Why that wicked man felt the need to walk through my sleep and into the back yard, truly puzzled me.

But I was in no shape to study the dream. It took more strength than I imagined to survive the coming days at work. Several friends had told me to stay busy. They said it was the best thing to do when suffering such a loss. Really? How could they know? How could anyone possibly imagine what this felt like if they hadn't experienced it themselves?

Yes, I was busy at work, but I was no-where near my A-game. The second I drove into work, Chip was there. The moment I walked into my office, Chip was there. He was everywhere I turned, but nowhere to be found. I didn't want to be there. I didn't want to be anywhere.

What I wanted more than anything was to sink beneath the ground to hide and to cry. To grieve. To die. I wanted to die. I wanted to be where Chip was… not here.

It became important to keep my wits in-tact at work and not cry if at all possible. Bills had to get paid and I *had* to work in order to do that. Being strong was not a tailor-made suit designed for me, yet I did it to move forward through the hours of horror. When I left one particular hell, I entered into the next. I was living two different lives surrounded by Chip.

And neither of them understood what I was suffering.

Everyday I'd get in the car to drive home and cry the entire way. I'd turn the corner and search for his truck, but it was never there. I'd pull in, put the car in park, and then sit for hours, crying. I didn't know any other way.

I screamed. I bawled until the tears soaked my clothes. I was a mess and very sick. I couldn't eat. I couldn't talk. There was nothing neither I nor anyone else could do to make me feel any better.

What was sinking in was only the beginning stages of understanding he wasn't coming home. And knowing he'd never walk through the front door ever again—the same door I stared at every day, wishing hard for him to re-appear.

My eyes were pitiful. The rivers of tears left a terrifying mark. My weary mind was exhausted but sleep refused to be at my beck and call. Even though I made it through the hours, alive, I couldn't see past the next minute. There was no tomorrow, no next week, no next year, no next anything.

I was dead inside.

That evening, I worried about falling asleep, not sure if I'd see that wicked man again. I had to convince myself, once again, that the only thing to fear was fear itself. I laid my heavy head down, wrapped my arms around Chip's pillow, and prayed out loud for him to be okay.

I pray to you my Lord, please keep Chip safe and let him be okay. I'm so worried about him. Please let him be okay.

The tears surged across my face and splattered onto the covers. I sobbed until sleep smothered my broken heart.

And then … I heard someone laughing.

Out of nowhere, an intense feeling of happiness danced right through me. It was so strong and so uplifting.

I hadn't a care in the world.

My ears were instantly filled with the sound of Chip's undeniable laughter. When I turned to look, he was there, standing beside me. His head was thrown back, his mouth was wide open, his arms were high up in the air, and he was laughing uncontrollably. He looked so unbelievably happy.

Suddenly, the tangible essence of love was tumbling in from the top of my head and dusting my entire body. It was warm and intimate; it was the perfect formula of Chip and Lyn combined.

We were holding hands. At the beach. Heading away from the ocean's edge. The waves crashed loudly and mixed beautifully with his laughter—it was a private orchestra made for one. I'd never experienced such peace before... it felt so, so good to be me.

Chip's laughter was highly contagious. If you were with him, you couldn't help it, you were laughing, too. It was second nature and sometimes I had no idea why I was chuckling.

The sand was very thick and hard to walk through. We would fall, get back up, only to tumble again. Keeping our voices to a low whisper was extremely problematic, but oh, so funny. The sand was stuck to my legs. When we reached the boardwalk, I tried to wipe it away but it was impossible to remove.

"We need to find a shower," Chip blurted.

In the blink of an eye, he turned and darted off. I quickly followed behind. A few feet away he opened the door to a small shop and entered. When he did, my eyes scurried across his body. He was wearing dark, navy blue, board shorts and no shirt. We were both barefoot.

And then, I noticed a few patrons walking about shopping.

"Do you guys have showers in here?" Chip asked. He was very loud. I was embarrassed for him but as usual, he didn't seem to mind.

"No," someone faraway yelled.

We both turned to walk away. Before I reached the door, I looked back to see if he was close. He was, but he had stopped and was now wearing a different expression on his face.

Chip was sporting a huge smile.

Out of the blue, he started laughing again, this time louder than before. It filled the shop from every angle and bounced around like loud thunder. Suddenly, his expression changed again. He took on a look of complete concentration—of strain.

Please no...

He did it anyway. The sound of a loud, long, gas passing noise permeated the shop. Everyone was startled, even me. I could hear all the ewww's and all the oh's. He farted.

Chip's laughter was boisterous, I couldn't help myself. I did it. I laughed too. We immediately rushed out the door.

"You just can't do that, sweetie," I told him, as we skipped down the sidewalk. I looked up, waiting for him to respond.

His head dipped down as his eyes melted into mine. I was captivated by his large smile when I watched his lips move and heard his voice slip through my ears.

"Why not?" he asked.

My eyes popped open.

"I'm awake? In bed? That was a dream?" I rolled to see if Chip was there. He wasn't.

"But I just saw him. I talked to him. Didn't I?"

Because he felt so real and so alive, I felt very confused. "He's not dead!" I shouted. I looked at the clock. "Or is he?"

Chapter Nine

HE'S ALIVE

I laid confused, wondering if I was okay. That was the second dream in two days where each one had felt real. And vivid. It was so intense in fact, I'd swear they were more real than my physical life.

I had to ask myself, "Did I make it up? Did I do it to be close to Chip?" And then I answered, "But how could I make something like that up?"

I knew I'd never choose that setting. Especially the part about walking into a store to look for showers when I knew none existed to begin with. To top it off, I would never, *ever*, want him to pass gas. That wasn't one of Chip's better attributes to begin with.

No, I knew I'd never design a dream such as that. Chip would though, it was so him. Once I concluded it was him, I then asked myself, "How'd he do that? More importantly, why'd he do that?"

Why am I thinking this way? Why am I thinking he's alive?

"Is there an afterlife?" I had finally proposed *the* question.

I knew nothing about the process of death or anything about an afterlife. I watched a few programs in the past about mediumship, but I never gave death a second thought. Why would I?

The only death I had ever experienced was my brother, Billy's. He committed suicide shortly after I turned twenty-one.

His funeral was the only one I had ever attended. I suppose it set the stage for my future because I avoided funerals like the plague. Now I knew why. They symbolized the end. The end of life as I knew it—Chip's service was only my second.

What was I supposed to believe?

On one hand, the dream filled me with mountains of love. We laughed and played like we always did. In one respect, he was showing me he was still alive in that other place called *the afterlife*.

Yet, on the other hand, I knew I couldn't allow myself to get sucked up inside of a dream world. It was complicated enough living in this physical one, I couldn't imagine living in both. Besides, I couldn't bring myself to believe there was something else other than human life.

The thing I hated the most was journeying through the motions of life. If Chip was unable to talk or laugh, I wasn't going to talk or laugh either. If he wasn't able to smile, if he couldn't show love, if he wasn't allowed to hug—it wasn't fair to him if I showed any semblance of compassion whatsoever. His sudden death was my official sadness. I was determined to wear his tragedy proudly.

Life sucked. And I wanted no part of it.

However, losing everything I owned wasn't a viable option either. I had to work. If I didn't, everything would eventually disappear. If I couldn't feed the kids, they'd starve. If I didn't crawl out of bed, I'd lose myself forever.

It took every ounce of energy to get myself to the office. But one morning, I was met with an unusual surprise. One that would eventually soar me into the realm of another world.

A co-worker raced through the doors and ran to my office.

"Lyn, Lyn, I have to tell you something," he shouted. His

pitch was unusually high. He had my undivided attention.

"I had a dream about Chip last night and it was so freaking weird." His hands were waving all around his head as he shared his excitement. He tried to sit but bounced right back up.

"I was still here at work and you girls were already gone for the day. The phone rang so I had to answer it," he said. He reached for the phone on the empty desk and placed it next to his ear.

"When I did, Chip was on the other end of the phone and he said, 'Hey man.'"

Goose bumps instantly covered my arms. Chip always said *hey man* to his friends. My co-worker couldn't possibly have known he said that to everyone.

He placed the phone on the desk and said, "All of a sudden, everything changes and I'm no longer here in the plant. I'm right in front of Chip and he's lying in a hospital bed. There's a white bandage wrapped around his head, but he's not hooked up to anything. When I glanced around the room, I saw nothing except the bed. And everything was extremely white. The walls were white, the floors were white—everything was *so* white."

He looked confused, "What I remember most, Lyn, is when we were talking back and forth, our lips weren't moving. It was like we were talking telepathically, you know?"

I nodded my head and watched him take a deep breath.

"Chip kept repeating over and over, 'I just wanted to say hi. Tell everyone I'm okay and thanks for everything.' And I kept telling him, 'That's great man. I'm glad you're okay and we can't wait for you to get better so you can come back to work.' And then he said it again, 'Tell everyone I said *Hi* and thanks for everything.'"

"I could hear my alarm going off in the background, but I

couldn't figure out where the sound was coming from. When I woke up, I didn't know if I was dreaming or if what had happened was real. I swear to you, Lyn, it felt real."

He looked down at the floor, scratched his head, and said, "It took me a few minutes to figure it all out. Yeah, that was crazy. I had to come in and tell you as soon as I got here."

He shuffled off but under his breath he whispered, "That was freaking wild." I agreed. I had never been so glued to someone's words as I was to his. I burned every single syllable he spoke onto a magical CD in my head.

He had no idea, but I knew exactly what he felt and understood it completely. What was so thrilling was that an outsider had just described an experience that felt real, like mine did.

I'll be darned, Chip was visiting from another world. Through dreams, he was sending messages—signals of sorts.

He had to be alive. There had to be an afterlife.

"But why would he visit this guy?" I asked myself.

The two of them weren't close but their personalities were quite similar. They were both loud and they both carried the same kind of verbal characteristics—sailor mouths.

Chip loved his job; maybe he visited this guy because of their work connection. Between owning his own business and working at the plant, he was living his dream. He felt safe and at home.

In his words, *I feel like I'm part of the family here.*

Regardless of the why, I was now faced with an important question: Did I discard everything that was happening, or was I supposed to believe in the dreams?

Well, that was an easy question to answer.

Discard the dreams.

Questioning my own sanity was becoming an everyday

occurrence. The last thing I needed was for someone else to question it, too. I had enough problems dealing with Chip's murder. Adding insanity to my plate wasn't needed.

"Besides, who believes in dreams?" I asked myself.

I certainly didn't.

Living in a dream world with my dead fiancé … how insane would that be?

Chapter Ten

GETTING NOTICED

There was nothing that remained the same except for taking care of our kids. Everything was getting worse... not better.

I had neither the energy nor the desire to do anything. I had nothing inside that remotely resembled who I was merely weeks ago. I was gone. I had died, too. I didn't laugh. I didn't smile. There was literally nothing... not even a glimmer of something.

My life had been altered and I hated being stuck inside my body. I cried constantly. And I begged Chip repeatedly, day after day, to take me away.

I need to be with you, Chip. You have to let me come and be with you. Please. I can't stand it here without you. I can't do this anymore, my love. Please, please, please... come and get me.

But I couldn't stop the new days from approaching. Before I knew it, another week had passed. It was getting increasingly clearer that I wasn't going to be allowed to be with Chip.

I didn't give much thought to the idea of an afterlife either. I was too consumed with my sadness and despair. Even if he was alive somewhere else, seriously, how was he going to help me now?

I did notice a few new things though—happenings—that made me cock my head in wonder. They weren't huge displays with neon lights, but I couldn't help but wonder if they were subtle hints of his continued survival.

The other day, the girls left for lunch and I stayed behind. I was sitting at my desk, alone in my office, with my back facing the door to the entrance.

I heard the door open, but I didn't turn to acknowledge that person's presence like I normally did. I was too engaged with my project and didn't want to lose my place.

Separating the driver lobby from my office was a long counter. From that counter came three loud knocks.

Knock—knock—knock.

I was a little irritated with the person's persistence, so I immediately turned around. At the same time, I asked this person, "How can I help...?" But I didn't finish the question. There was no one standing there.

There was no one there.

I jumped from my chair and ran behind the counter. I figured someone was playing around and might be ducking.

Nope. There was no one there.

I slowly walked to my desk and sat there with a puzzled mind. Did I make this up too? Am I dreaming this? I pinched myself hard—hard enough to know I wasn't dreaming.

Okay. So what do I do with this? Do I acknowledge something happened I can't answer? Do I acknowledge this was Chip, saying hello?

Or do I continue to be my skeptical self and bury this deep in my mind and give it no relevance whatsoever.

Yep, I bury it ... for now.

Chapter Eleven

HARD ANSWERS

T he hours sitting in my car upon my arrival home—they remained the same. Releasing the stream of tears that built up behind my eyes everyday became a necessity.

I sat talking to a dead man. One I couldn't see, hear, or feel. I told him everything. Sometimes I reasoned with him. Sometimes I looked up into the sky and asked God, "Why Chip?" Sometimes I cussed the world, but mostly, I dove head-first into a sorrow that never went away.

And then, one day something amazing happened. It was a Tuesday morning when I rolled over to Chip's side of the bed and hugged his pillow. I wanted to lie there a few more minutes before I had to fight another horrible day. I closed my eyes tightly and waited for time to pass.

Suddenly, it felt like someone took their thumb and forefinger and used them to gently pinch my behind. There wasn't a doubt in my mind—my butt had been grabbed and pinched.

My eyes shot open. I didn't move. Not an inch.

But I did smile. For the first time in weeks—I actually smiled. I didn't think I'd ever do that again.

"Good morning, my love," I whispered.

It could be no other. It was exactly something Chip would do; grab, rub, or pinch my behind. He did it all the time. This couldn't be a figment of my imagination. I rolled over and questioned it, "Or could it? I didn't make that up, right?" But there was no one to answer. Sleeping was over. I jumped out of bed and searched for him everywhere. But Chip was no-where to be found.

What the hell am I doing? Am I going crazy?

I had no choice. Several minutes later, I convinced myself I had made it up. The way I figured—I was somehow able to create the madness I was experiencing. When someone loses their mind, unexplainable things can happen. As for me, I was convinced I had begun the stages of insanity.

How could I not be crazy... a dead man was talking to me.

Undoubtedly, I was being pushed into seeing the existence of an afterlife. However, I seemed to take great pride in doubting it. As soon as I doubted it though, something else would happen.

Later that same day...

I was on my computer at work trying to complete my morning invoicing. Located on my desk to the right of me was a calculator. I always kept it in the *on* position, but rarely used it. Out of nowhere, it operated like it was in the *printing* mode, but I had never put paper in it.

Yet, there it was—running—printing without paper—while my fingers remained on the computer keyboard, typing. I stared at the calculator in complete bewilderment. I couldn't fathom how or why it was doing what it was doing. And then, it stopped. Just like that.

I sat vacantly. No thoughts. I had nothing.

I was in a complete blanket of shock. When out of nowhere, the lights flickered, the computer blinked, and everything went dark. Everything shut down.

The lights returned a few minutes later; however, the entire computer system had crashed. For hours. With nothing else to do, I traveled a new direction of thought.

Is it possible he's trying to show me he's not gone? Is it possible he did all of this today?

"It is possible, isn't it?"

Did I dare step out of my comfort zone and enter something unknown to take a tour into the Afterlife—something I knew nothing about?

I wasn't sure I could do that. But if he was still alive, I desperately needed to talk to him. I needed to know he was okay. I knew at that moment I had to find a way to start studying the Afterlife.

Yet knowing it and doing it were two entirely different beasts. The sadness inside weighed so much more than the curiosity. It was only week four and I still had no energy to do anything but cry.

I searched the internet for upcoming events, and surprisingly, I purchased a ticket to a Sylvia Browne event. She was a world-famous psychic medium who appeared regularly on *The Montel Williams Show*.

The venue was sold out and all I had to do was wait for the date to arrive. I had no clue why I had bought the ticket, especially one to see a medium. It was unlike anything I'd ever done. I hadn't an answer for that either.

Meanwhile, in my other life, more questions emerged about the morning of Chip's murder. His mom and I would go over, second by second, everything that happened that morning, trying to figure it all out. How it happened seemed to be the mystery we couldn't solve.

There were unanswered questions like, what time was he actually shot? Was it 4:45 a.m. or was it 4:46 a.m.? What time did the perpetrator get there before Chip arrived? How long did he wait for him? What kind of gun was used?

The detectives were tight-lipped, sharing very little. Having the answers certainly wouldn't bring any kind of peace, it certainly wouldn't bring Chip back, yet somehow it became a statement of sorts to locate answers.

To be honest, I think it gave us something to do. Something to focus on while we waited for news. Besides, whatever we came up with was pure conjecture. We knew nothing of the evidence to substantiate fact from fiction.

While we searched though, something mysterious occurred. It happened on a Friday morning when I found myself lying in bed, drenched in confusion. I didn't know what to make of it. The dream that is. I had awakened from another odd dream.

I knew I witnessed something amazing but I couldn't believe it. It was more vivid, more real, than any movie I'd ever seen. It felt like I went outside, hopped in the car with Chip, and he took us for a ride. It was that real.

We were driving our Infiniti back to the dealership where we purchased it. Chip wanted the floor mats in the rear to be replaced. I didn't know why, but he was pretty adamant about it.

I was standing beside Chip, watching him talk to the representative. All of my attention was vested into their conversation. My head literally bounced back and forth as I listened to each one of them discuss the mats.

I decided to get nosy and walked over and opened the rear driver-side door. I put my knee on the seat and leaned down to the floor, examining the mats. There wasn't a thing wrong with either one of them; they looked brand new.

Why in the world are we getting new mats? I questioned.

"I want these replaced," I heard Chip say again, "They have to be brand new and those are not."

The man didn't argue. He was willing to satisfy Chip's

demands. The rep walked away when Chip and I were left alone, standing by the car, side-by-side.

He looked directly at me, and then deeply into my eyes. His stare was hypnotizing. It was undeniable that whatever he was thinking or whatever he was about to say, he wanted me to pay attention.

He leaned in and whispered, "350."

I looked over at the car but instantly swung my head back around. "No. 349," I said.

My eyes charged open.

I was wide awake and in the blink of an eye, it was all gone. Paralyzed, I laid very confused. "What's happening to me?" I screamed out. I was worried now. But as fast as I was filled with concern, I was also filled with curiosity.

What did that mean? Was it a precursor to the 350 and the 349 comment? It has to be. Okay, so what does it mean? 350; is this the gun or is this a time? 349; this can't be a gun, so it has to be a time. What if it's both?

Motionless, I laid wondering if the gun used to kill Chip was a 3.50. And then I wondered if the 3:49 a.m. was the time his perpetrator arrived at the scene and waited for him to arrive.

Is it possible he sent two answers in one dream?

Regardless of the correct answer, I found it interesting. I knew there was a definite meaning. When he looked that deeply into my eyes—he wanted me to hear him.

"This is important, Lyn," I told myself. "Don't forget it."

But as soon as I hopped out of bed, I sunk right back into that skeptic creature living inside.

"What's wrong with you? You know better. You know you can't believe in dreams," I yelled.

"But why not?" I had a knack for talking to myself now.

I had seen TV shows about mediums and the afterlife before. If I thought it was possible then, why couldn't it be possible now?

"It can happen, right?" This time I was asking for a sign. A voice. Anything to let me know I wasn't cracking up.

But I heard nothing outside of my own breathing.

I was so confused. I was roaming between two worlds. The real life world and a dream world now. I seriously didn't know what to believe.

What I did know for certain was—Chip wasn't here anymore. I knew without a shadow of doubt he was never coming back home and I would never see him again. I found it impossible to get past the *why*. And the crying—it never ended. It was physically handicapping me.

My heart was ripping with the continued pain and its power—it was so much more powerful than the mystery of the new experiences.

The communications via dreams and signs came, I relished in the magic of their puzzling mystery—but only for a short time. My mind found a way to cover them all up with the hurtful pain that never went away.

If Chip was trying to communicate, I wasn't listening.

My ears, my eyes, my mind … all closed to the path he wanted me to see.

Chapter Twelve

I'M OKAY

I still couldn't believe he was dead. I was heading into the fifth week and I was no better off than week one. I was losing grip on all reality.

Each day I found myself confessing that something very serious was wrong with me. I was overwhelmed with the aspects of physical life and then this something else I couldn't explain as well.

Chip was showing up in my head almost every night. I didn't know which way to turn or how to separate the two worlds. Sadly, I felt better sleeping. It was my only escape. Not just from the outside world, but from my mind as well. It was simple there. I lived more in the moment instead of constantly thinking like I did when I was awake.

Every night I soaked my pillow with tears, always expecting to fall asleep minutes later. But this one evening something different happened. Before a single tear had the chance to appear, I found myself standing outside under the morning sun.

"I don't remember getting up this morning. Oh no, now I'm losing time too? This isn't good."

Standing outside the door of my office with the other girls, we stared out into the large yard in front of us. Chip was busy packing up his pickup truck.

He was removing things from a small shed and then putting it into his red truck. It was clear he was packing up to leave.

The two of us had a mutual agreement—we didn't speak at

work. Because of this, I stood beside the other girls and watched. I wanted to go over to him, but I didn't want the gossip that could possibly go with it.

"Get your butt over there and go talk to him," my friend said. I nodded my head, smiled, and walked fast. When I approached Chip, I noticed him talking to my sister.

Before I got close enough to touch him, he turned and headed back to his truck. I knew he saw me, but he didn't walk up to me.

My arms spread wide open, I shouted to my sister, "The love of my life hasn't even acknowledged me yet." I watched the tears well up in her eyes but I didn't question why she cried. Instead, I walked past her and headed toward Chip.

I tagged along directly behind him, watching his every move from the shed to his truck. He stopped and placed a box on the ground and only then did he turn to face me. I positioned my right hand on top of his chest and looked up into his blue eyes.

I whispered, "I've been so worried about you, my love."

He grabbed me and hugged me tightly.

And then he said, "I'm okay, baby doll. But you didn't have to leave your number."

"I didn't know what else to do," I told him.

I wasn't sure what he meant by his comment, but I didn't care. He was there holding me. I could feel him and see him.

"I know," he whispered in my ear. He held me tighter. "It's all right, baby doll. Everything's all right."

"Where are you going? Aren't you coming back to work?"

"No, darlin, I really must go."

"Go where? Where are you going?" I asked.

But he wouldn't answer.

Instead, he kept packing. A few minutes later as he placed another box on the floor, I saw a small bandage on top of his *head. His hair was cut much shorter. Like a crew cut. I tried to remember the last time we went to the salon, but nothing came to mind.*

He took a break after placing another box in the truck. I tried hard to think of something to say to make him change his mind. I didn't want him to leave. But just as I was about to say something, he moved away.

He reached inside the truck and grabbed a hand towel from the front seat. I watched him as he wiped the sweat from his forehead and then across the bandage on top of his head. It was clear he wanted me to see the bandage—the size of a Band-Aid—but he made no comment about it. And neither did I.

A few minutes later, he finished packing. We were standing beside the truck, side-by-side, when my sister walked up and put food in the back seat for him, for his trip. When she did, he leaned forward and placed a cold bottle against her leg. She jumped around and yelped.

Chip belted out a thunderous belly laugh. He laughed so loud and so hard—I couldn't help it; I laughed too. He was such a goober.

But then suddenly, I heard a loud noise coming from out of nowhere. I looked up when everything turned dark—the noise didn't end. It almost sounded as though it were coming from somewhere inside of my head.

Tap—tap—tap. Three times, loudly.

My eyes shot open.

I was wide awake and scared out of my wits. Someone had tapped on something and they were inside my house; I was sure of it. I scanned the bedroom, searching. But there was no one there.

It took a few minutes to calm myself down. To calm my

heartbeat and to also realize—I only heard the loud tapping from inside of my head, not from my bedroom. Several minutes later I felt comfortable enough to go back to sleep. It was only midnight. Too early to get up.

"I hear a song. Where's that coming from?" I asked, while I searched around. Everything was pitch black but a glorious melody could be heard. It was a song by The Carpenters.

~Why do birds, suddenly appear, every time, you are near. Just like me, they long to be, close to you.~

The music was playing all around me. From every angle, so clear, so gentle like, and so beautiful, it fused the very air that I breathed. Like a soft blanket of harmony wrapped around my body, it cradled me like a baby.

Suddenly, a soft light appeared below when I was allowed to see the ground. Its exterior looked bumpy and rocky, rough in texture. I was getting closer to it. But not fast. I was swaying, back and forth, slowly, floating.

"Am I in the air?" I asked myself.

And then I answered, "Yes, I'm floating."

With each swaying motion, the ground appeared smoother. And the song, it was getting further and further away yet the words could still be heard...

~ Just like me, they long to be, close to you.~

By the time I reached the dirty ground, it was completely smoothed out; no rough spots anywhere. And the Karen Carpenter song, it had all but disappeared.

Tap—tap—tap.

My head bounced to the side.

I heard it again. Loudly.

My eyes flew open—for the second time.

I was startled and once more, I searched the room but saw no one there. I tried staying calmer this time. Freaking out only made my heart beat fast and loud inside my head. I laid back down and focused on breathing instead. Soon, I closed my eyes. Before I knew it…

I was looking at a metal object.

"What? Where am I?" I asked myself.

The metal object was literally stuck in front of my eyes. I studied it hard but I couldn't make it out. It was silver in color and looked like metal. Then it grew. Bigger and rounder all at the same time. It was so close I could reach out and touch it— but I didn't. It reminded me of the side of an airplane; the part of the wing maybe.

"Whoa, I'm flying," I shouted.

Just like that, I was flying. Instinctively I knew Chip was holding me, gliding us through time. The wind ruffled through my hair, flapping it all over my face, blinding me. And then suddenly, I saw water below. The breeze was no more. We were suspended, floating in place, watching the ocean whip wildly up and over a seawall.

The moon was gleaming and when I lifted my head, I gasped. The tips of the waves glistened from the bright light above, dancing crazily in its dramatic but synchronistic performance. It was magnificent. And that sound of the waves crashing—so hypnotic, majestic, full of mystery.

Time was no longer a factor. For hours it seemed, we floated in place gazing at the beauty. But then, my curiosity decided to march forward.

"Is this where the gun was thrown, my love?" I blurted.

There was no answer.

Instead, I was whisked away from the beauty. In a flash, like the genie blinking her eyes in "I Dream of Jeannie", we were there. Drifting ever so slowly—over a tributary.

And then zoom, we were off again. I could see the canals

flying by. Zoom, we were flying through another. Zoom, and then another.

"*This is so much fun,*" I screamed out.

I was having the time of my life. I was always into going fast, but this was utterly fantastic, and so much faster than the speed of Superman. We were zooming.

The lights that glowed along the canals—they sparkled like little stars dancing across the water, blinking as we past them by.

Tap—tap—tap.

My eyes bolted open, again.

I was wide awake.

I laid there, frozen, staring a hole straight into the ceiling, in shock. "Wow. What was all of that?" I yelled.

But of course, no one answered me.

"What are you doing to me, Chip?"

I questioned my sanity briefly and then rapidly dismissed everything I was questioning. I was being sucked right up into a dream world. It was becoming clearer now. What I was experiencing wasn't going to be easy to explain.

It was so freaking real.

Is it normal to experience these kinds of dreams? Is this what other people go through too when they lose a loved one? This must be normal, it just has to be.

Several minutes had passed while I lay in a cloud of complete wonder. I went over every detail marking it vividly in my mind.

And then I asked out loud, "What exactly are you trying to show me, sweetie?"

He gave me nothing more—except silence …

Chapter Thirteen

MAGIC DAY

Today was the day. It was Sylvia Browne day. I didn't understand why I needed to go; I only knew that I had to. Hearing something from Chip was a given, but I also knew the likelihood of that happening was slim to none.

My main goal? To stop feeling like I was going insane.

I didn't get away from work as early as I wanted. With no time to change clothes, I wore what I had on—one of Chip's Gator sweat shirts. It was his Christmas present but he never got the chance to wear it.

I drove the Infiniti downtown, located a parking spot about a block from the auditorium, and headed inside. It took a while to find my seat—it was located far up in the nosebleed section. If it weren't for the huge TV screen on stage, I imagine I would've seen nothing.

When I entered the building, I was given a band with an embedded number to wrap around my wrist. I was told if Sylvia called that number at the end of her show, I'd be allowed to ask her *one* question. Since I'd never been to an event like this, I considered myself a newbie, soaking it all in.

The venue was to be over around 9:30 p.m. and Sylvia showed up shortly after eight o'clock. She talked about the afterlife, about her personal life, she spoke about her tour, and she commercialized her books. Did I learn anything? Yes, and no.

What she explained wasn't anything I didn't already know.

And no, I had never read any of her books. I hadn't read any medium's books up to that point. What I was interested in— what I waited for—was for the numbers to be called. That's what I selfishly wanted to be a part of.

The time had arrived. She pulled numbers out of a basket, calling them out one at a time. Twenty in all. Mine wasn't one of them. She did say, however, if there was more time she would call more numbers to get in as many people as possible.

I was so tired. It was well past my bedtime, but I stayed. I bent over to pick up my water from the floor when the key to my car fell out of the pouch pocket of my shirt. I had a heck of a time finding it. I finally put it back inside and sat quietly listening to the show.

Sylvia went through twenty people rather quickly. She then told the audience she had enough time for seven more numbers. I had mine memorized.

I had thought of a question earlier if I got picked. It was going to go something like this: can you tell me if there were two shooters or only the one? Of course I would explain first that my fiancé was murdered and I didn't know how many were involved.

Yes. That was it. That was going to be my question.

It too, was memorized.

She called out five numbers. They weren't mine. I reached down to grab my purse and water when my key fell out again. I grabbed it up, and the rest of my belongings as well, preparing to leave. But then...

I heard it. She called out every single digit—of my number.

Oh — my — God! That's — my — number!

The auditorium was packed. Every seat filled. More than two thousand people in attendance. And there I was, walking down a set of stairs to ask the one and only Sylvia Browne a question about my dead fiancé. My heart was literally beating out of my chest I was so nervous.

"Geesh Lyn, calm down," I told myself.

With shaking knees I stood at the mic. It was my turn.

"Hi Sylvia."

"Hello," she said in a deep voice. "What is your question?"

My mouth opened, "What happens to souls if they've been taken by the hands of another?"

What? What? Noooo! That's not your question. Why did you ask that? Where the hell did that come from? Sssshhh!

"Well, it depends," she said. "If they're in shock, they will go into a cocoon state and stay there until they have healed for at least a year or so."

The instructions were very clear. Ask only *one* question. But my lips parted and the words escaped.

"I don't think he's in a cocoon. I think he has visited me several times already."

She went silent for a few seconds.

"Yes, he has," she confirmed. "And he will continue to do so. You haven't heard the last from him. I promise."

"Okay, thank you." It was the first time I heard my voice echo through the large auditorium. I wanted so badly to ask more. But I knew it wasn't fair to everyone else.

So I turned from the microphone and walked down the stairs. I didn't quite understand why I asked what I did, but it didn't matter now. I was on top of the world, and still couldn't believe my number had been called.

Several of Sylvia's books were for sale on a nearby table. I stopped and bought, *Temples on the Other Side*, and then proceeded to my car with a new outlook on this entire experience. This experience that Chip was sharing.

Once I learned that the numbers were going to be called, I

asked him for a favor… silently that is, in my mind.

I sort of whispered it to him.

I said, "If you're still alive Chip, please have my number called."

Did he make it happen? I believe he did.

Chapter Fourteen

IT DOESN'T HAVE TO END

A s I drove home from the show, I couldn't help but acknowledge that my curiosity was developing into an enormous hill of hope. It was becoming a mission and one I knew I had to sink myself into.

If anything, I knew I had to search for answers. My desire? To make sure that Chip was okay. The mission—to learn, hear, and see Chip, wherever he may be.

If he was real, if he still existed, if he was indeed alive, I needed to know. The only way I perceived to learn, was to read. I had to study on a subject I gave little consideration to. Sure I had a passing thought here or there when it came to the afterlife, but nothing serious.

And then I remembered something. I drifted back in time to a moment where the afterlife was actually discussed.

Chip and I spent our time during Christmas vacation riding around the west side of Jacksonville. We searched endlessly for our first home. Taking our time felt natural since we wanted the most perfect one.

One evening though, we stayed in and I decided to get laundry done. I was headed to the back of the house while the kids sat with their dad watching TV. I made it a few steps past where they sat, when I stopped dead in my tracks.

I had the most powerful sense of having already walked through that very moment before. I quickly turned toward Chip.

"Déjà vu," I shouted.

"You've been having a lot of those lately," he said.

"I know, right? I've never had so many in such a short period of time." This one included, we counted five in the last two days. Instead of heading to the laundry room, I walked over and sat on top of the coffee table directly in front of him.

I unexpectedly blurted, "Do you believe in life after death?"

It came out of nowhere. I was just as shocked as he was. The look he possessed was priceless though. He stared at me in astonishment, complete bewilderment. But I didn't budge. I stared back. My eyes were locked to his while I waited patiently for a response.

"No," he said.

Okay, but that's not what I'm looking for.

And yet, I had no idea what I was searching for or why I had asked such a weird question to begin with. For some ungodly reason, I felt freakishly determined to discuss this topic. I asked again—in a different way.

"So you don't think there's a possibility we continue to exist after we die?"

"No, I don't," he answered too fast. I wasn't sure what to say next, so I averted my eyes and looked at the floor.

"But," he began, and my eyes lifted. "If you're asking me if I believe something else exists besides us, then yes, I do believe that."

He leaned around me, turned down the TV, and placed Scooby on the floor. I was fixated now and couldn't wait for him to continue.

"I've watched that show a few times with Mom…"

I interrupted, "John Edwards?"

"Yes, that's him. I can see where people believe in that kind of stuff, but that's not for me. I'm the kind of person who has to see something before I believe it. You have to show me, like stick it right here in front of my face." He lifted his hand in front of his nose. "I need to see it with my own eyes. And then maybe I'll believe it."

"What is it that you believe exists besides us?" I asked.

His silence scared me, but only because I didn't want him to feel like I was invading his personal thoughts.

"Aliens. I believe aliens are right here with us, as well as out there," he said.

I was stunned.

The tone of his voice was so authoritative—there was no mistaking how much he believed his statement. There was no hesitation in the conversation either. I felt like I knew exactly what he was suggesting.

"Roswell exists, doesn't it?" (As in Roswell UFO Project)

"Yes. And others, too," he said, nodding his head.

"Others, too?" I had slipped up. Taken by surprise, I had found it hard to believe.

I knew better than to ask about things he did in the Navy. Years ago, I learned to stop asking him questions about his military career. Much of his time was spent under secrecy and he told me a hundred times, *I'm not allowed to talk about it.*

My mind was twirling though. I knew he could see it.

"It's like the Bible, darlin—do you believe in the Bible?" he asked. He had turned the table on me; it was so like him. Yet, my mouth moved before I had a chance to think it out.

"I believe the prophets wrote their works, yes. But I also believe many years ago man deleted important elements that were written. I believe they erased history that was meant to be shared. Why do you ask?"

"Because I believe the Bible is based on interpretation. Everything you read is all in how you perceive it and interpret it. Does God exist? I don't know. I guess I'll find that out when my number's up. But I don't believe I should believe in something that has been written by man. God is not a man, he's a Higher Power. And man has a tendency to exaggerate and lie. The Bible is written by man, no matter if they are considered prophets or not. They are still of the human flesh. They are man."

"No argument there, sweetie," I assured him.

"So, do you believe in the Bible and every word that's written in it?" he asked it again.

Wow, how do I answer that?

I was vehemently searching for the right answer but instead, my mind jumped off into a completely different direction.

"Do you remember me telling you about that book I read last year, *The DaVinci Code?*" I asked.

"Yes, I do. I remember your confusion with a dispute about *The Last Supper*, right?"

"Yes, that's right," I was elated he remembered. "And the way DaVinci depicted Mary Magdalene in the painting." He nodded his head in agreement, smiling, almost like he knew where this was all going. "What I don't understand was the importance of keeping her a secret."

I took a breath, "She was also a prophet, yet her writings weren't included in the Bible, along with others, I know. But she was a woman. What I interpret is that the Church chose what they wanted to have read and believed in. And that didn't include her, her devotion, her loyalty to Jesus, her work or her writings. That's not telling the truth. And when truths are hidden, then questions arise. Me, personally, I question how much truth is written. Does that make sense?"

"It makes perfect sense," he said. "With anything you read, my love, not just the Bible, it's all in how your mind interprets what you read. Either you're going to believe it or you're going to question it and have your doubts. You bring up Mary Magdalene—in the movie *The Passion of the Christ*—she was right there by Mother Mary's side, wiping up his blood, and was at his feet by the cross too; remember?"

"Yes." I had no clue where he was headed.

"The movie showed her being a prostitute, but it also showed her loyalty to Jesus Christ. I think in today's time, people are beginning to question more. They want to know what else is there that they haven't been allowed to see."

"Do you believe in Jesus Christ?" I asked. I thought he might hesitate on this one, but he didn't.

"I believe he existed, yes. Do I believe he was resurrected? That falls back into the same category we began with. I have to see it, to believe it."

Scooby began raising all kinds of noise at the door. We both laughed, and then I jumped up to let him out. After Scooby and I returned, my focus went back to laundry.

That subject never came up again.

Three weeks later he was dead.

Those few moments in time baffled me. I never thought about life after death. And what's really odd, is how I sat myself in front of him demanding he give me an answer. I would never do that, but I did it, that one evening.

Looking back, I'd swear my thoughts were interfered with and replaced with a freakish determination. Chip had a rule when it came to our topic of conversations. No politics and no religion. He told me years ago those two topics would kill a relationship. I laughed when he said it, but I agreed to oblige. Since we never discussed religion, I knew I would never ask him about an afterlife.

I wish now I would have paid attention to the signals

though, the signs. That night, in my opinion, was a huge sign. If I'd had the wherewithal to recognize it as a spiritual sign, I have to wonder if I could have changed the outcome of our lives.

Reality kicked back in. I was home, pulling into the driveway. I had my new book in my hands, eager to dig in. I knew I wouldn't wait until tomorrow—how could I? I was still floating on top of a big high believing Chip had his hand in getting my number called.

I took care of the kids, spent a little time with them, put them both to bed, and then ran to my room. After placing Chip's pillow in front of mine, I leaned back and lifted up the book.

I began to read…

While I scanned through the introduction I noticed something unusual—a familiar scent. It was the scent of *clean* that filled the entire bedroom. If I didn't know better, I'd swear Chip's clothes were laid out across the bed. I loved that smell. He always smelled like he came straight from a warm dryer.

Hanging tightly to my newfound hope system, I lowered the book to my lap and spoke out loud to an invisible man.

"I know you are here, my darling. I love you so much."

I waited for something to happen but after a few minutes of nothing, and the scent vanishing, I raised the book and read through the first chapter.

Since I had to work the next day, I put the book away and laid my head down. Never missing one single night, I told him how much I loved him and how badly I missed him.

Instantly, the dark sadness rose from deep inside and surfaced into tears. But tonight, I was exhausted. With no warning whatsoever, I was walking on a beach…

"I don't remember driving out here," I said to myself,

"When did we do that?" I could see it was dark out, late into the evening. I could hear the waves crashing so I knew where I was.

And then, I felt my head resting against Chip's chest—my lover was here and in an instant, every worry was erased. His arm was wrapped tightly around me, holding me close as we slowly, very slowly, strolled along the moonlit beach.

It felt so good to be me.

Chip's love was encapsulating me. Happiness was fused to my very essence. I could touch it, feel it, taste it—I was in love with love and floating high on calmness and serenity.

In order to catch the strength of Chip's love embracing me physically, my heart had to skip two beats. His love was literally pouring strongly from his soul.

The wind was whipping my hair while I listened to the waves crashing beside us. They were merely feet away. And then I felt it—a solid kiss on the top of my head.

I leaned back and looked up. Softly, he kissed my head three times. I smiled and then he leaned in and kissed the tip of my nose. When his lips touched mine—I kissed him back.

Everything was exactly as it should be. I rested my head against his chest again and enjoyed the slow walk to nowhere. His hand gently caressed my bottom, my sure sign of his love.

Minutes later, he whispered close to my ear, "I don't want this night to end."

I lovingly said, "Me either, my love."

After a few more minutes, he jumped in front of me and grabbed my hand, pulling me quickly down the beach. I swore I felt "love" radiating from him. It was unquestionable; we wanted to be right there, right where we were.

Suddenly, I saw three enormous stones, at least twelve feet high; sitting side-by-side. They reminded me of Scotland's

Stonehenge. Chip released my hand, took off toward them, and then stood in the middle. It was a perfect Kodak moment. I wished I had my camera.

But then. he fumbled with his clothing. He reached out and pulled me close and laughingly whispered, "Look out for the people, sweetie. I have something to show you."

I laughed. I knew what he was thinking—he wanted to play. I stepped back a step and took a silent picture of him. His head was leaning to the side slightly, his eyes were sparkling blue, and his smile was simply stunning.

I smiled back—and fell in love all over again.

I darted wide awake.

Instantly, tears filled my eyes. I couldn't help it, I cried. I didn't want to; I didn't want Chip to think I was sad.

But it was *that* wonderful.

I rolled over, grabbed his pillow, and threw myself onto it. I openly confessed, "That was so beautiful, sweetie. That is so you and me. And always will be."

And then I cried with a force to complete breathlessness. It was so real. It was so alive. I wanted to be there with him.

Not here. Not here…

I never knew he was dead because he felt … so alive.

Chapter Fifteen

A BALL OF ENERGY

I spent all of my free time drenched in reading that book. It was the sixth week and amazingly, it was occupying a big part of my thoughts. I truly felt like I was learning something. In a positive way.

I was still crying. All the time. But not when I was reading. The tantrums certainly rocked my body, but my curiosity was getting the better of me.

That was probably a good thing.

The dreams were coming regularly. I began documenting them weeks earlier. They all seemed to carry a special message. If I was asking a question, it felt like the dream was there to give me an answer.

Can I receive messages inside of a dream?

I was starting to think I could.

For example: The question about *time* became paramount. Certainly I knew it wouldn't make me feel better, but I wanted to piece the events together in chronological order. I couldn't explain why. It was more of a need to know thing.

In my heart of hearts, I believed I had already received an answer pertaining to the arrival of the killer. According to a dream days ago, the time was 3:50 a.m. That was the time given by Chip inside of the dream.

Now I wanted to know what time the first shot was fired. It was narrowed down to either 4:45 a.m. or 4:46 a.m. According to my cell records and my memory of the events.

And then something unusual happened...

It was early in the morning. Normally, I woke from the alarm with a song blasting, but on this one day, I was awakened by something completely different.

Instead of hearing the alarm clock, I heard *words*.

"Four forty-five," the words said, loudly inside my head.

It was so loud in fact, it felt like a pounding headache but it had a number format hooked to it. And it kept pounding. One right after the other.

"Four forty-five. Four forty-five, four forty-five."

When my feet hit the floor, it vanished. It just stopped.

There it was. The answer to my question. Not that it was going to solve a darn thing, but it did open my eyes to something new.

Chip was talking to me... and it wasn't inside of a dream.

I thought about this occurrence all day.

I was thrilled to experience something different, yet I was weary at the same time. I wanted to believe Chip was still alive and a huge part of me did. There was just one small detail missing—no hard evidence.

My skeptic-self refused to part ways.

That same chilly evening I lay in bed and read my book. I perused a couple of chapters summarizing temples and halls on the other side. The one I was most fascinated by was called, *Hall of Reconnection.*

It was as it stated—a hall to reconnect with loved ones. I wanted to go there badly and connect with Chip. I knew if I could get myself there, and if he was really alive, he would meet me in that Hall.

I put the book down and laid in silence, thinking. Wondering if what I was doing was normal. Questioning if anyone else was experiencing this type of connection, and then deliberating whether I was losing my mind. But I gave in…

"Please come visit me in my dreams, Chip. I need to see you. If you can't come to me in my dreams, please meet me at the Hall of Reconnection."

And there it was. My first affirmation.

I set my intention and believed—*truly believed*—it would happen. I repeated it twice more, making doubly sure my thoughts were being heard. Chip's picture was sitting on the dresser and I stared at it for the longest time. Minutes later, I closed my eyes and then whispered.

"Chip, make me a believer."

The loneliness was seeping slowly through my veins. The emptiness still had its hold on me and took over in a second's notice. I truly missed him. I missed his touch, his scent; I missed getting lost inside of his eyes. Those blazing baby blues that showed me no one loved me the way that he did.

I cried until sleep took me away.

I woke up in the middle of the night.

When I came to, I was already sitting straight up in the bed, dazed. I didn't think it odd I was sitting up, not right then anyway. I sat there for a moment thinking and then turned to look at the floor. I saw something—glowing.

A big ball of light was traveling under my door entering my room, gliding slowly across the floor.

The ball of light vibrated brilliantly with beams of white light shining dazzlingly all around it. It was an intense white with the prettiest baby blue I'd ever seen.

Shaped like an oval watermelon, it had transparent columns. I was able to see right through it. All I could do was watch it though, float slowly across the floor. It didn't seem to be in a hurry to get anywhere fast.

The colors changed from white to blue, and then blue to

107

white, and then back to white to blue—a perfect vibrating relationship that pulsated somehow, vibrating together, loudly.

It seemed to know exactly where it was headed. When it reached the end of the bed, I felt an explosion of newfound beliefs rushing out.

"I know you're energy now, Chip," I shouted.

I couldn't believe I opened my mouth. But I had read somewhere recently we were all made up of energy. Our souls are energy. Our loved ones are as well. I guess I wanted to share that.

The ball of light disappeared but only for a second or two. Somehow it crawled up and appeared at the foot of the bed. It was still moving. Forward. Slowly. It never deviated its speed. It crawled like a snail right toward me.

I felt no fear though. I watched in awe and accepted whole heartedly it was Chip. I thought it might stop—but it didn't. It came closer, and closer, moving over my feet. And then over my legs. It crawled up my abdomen and when it reached my chest, the ball of light glided right in. Right inside of my chest.

I shouted, "Oh crap!"

In a flash, a jolting charge surged throughout my entire body all at once. It was electrifying. From the top of my head all the way to the tips of my toes—this unique electric charge was dancing inside of me.

I screamed out loud, "It just vanished inside of me. Oh no!"

The fear had finally kicked in.

I didn't have a clue what was happening and the unknown was very scary. But it didn't hurt. I was quivering with electricity, yes, but not in any kind of pain. It was more like I had been plugged in somewhere and the switch had been turned on.

I decided to lie back down.

I turned over on my side and stared at the facing wall. I wiggled my toes to see if the vibration would leave. It hadn't.

I convinced myself I needed to get back to sleep so that Chip could come and talk to me. While feeling the subtle vibrations dance inside, I closed my eyes and drifted into slumber.

Upon waking, I found myself very confused.

I couldn't for the life of me figure out if I was awake or asleep when that blue light entered my room, when it entered my body. Still to this day I'm not sure. What I did remember quite well though—I had purposely fluffed my pillow. I had to be awake.

I also wondered about something else too—what would anyone think if I shared this? I knew what I'd think: they're loony as hell. With that thought, it was easy to conclude that this had to stay a secret. If anyone knew I was communicating with my dead fiancé... I'd indeed be committed—or so I thought.

Later, I asked myself, "Did he make me a believer?"

My answer was simple. If I wasn't one yesterday, I was certainly one today.

Seeing is believing.

If he wasn't alive ... then I was definitely going crazy.

Chapter Sixteen

TAP, TAP, TAP

T *emples on the Other Side* was officially completed. My thoughts now ventured into the new unknown world of the Afterlife. I learned a little, but I knew I had so much more I needed to figure out. The mission wasn't completed. Far from it.

In 2008, the majority of books available were authored by famous mediums. I often wondered if they had an advantage I didn't possess. What if they really did see glimpses of the other side? What if they knew something I didn't?

If there was even the slightest truth from their words, then I wanted to grab as much knowledge as possible. I wanted an open mind. As wide open as I could get.

Besides, I didn't have a choice—not really. I was pulled in this direction, afterlife communications, and I didn't fully understand why at the time.

It was week seven and my mission was stronger than ever. All of my spare time was sunk into research. Anything I could get my hands on about the afterlife or paranormal experiences, I was reading it. If I wasn't reading a book, I was searching the internet.

At the time, I was unable to locate anything that directly related to what I was experiencing. Or, I failed to search in the right places. Most of the books were stories about the clients of mediums, not their own experiences. It didn't matter though. I had to learn. So I purchased books by, *Allison Dubois, John*

Edwards, James VanPraugh, and others.

I felt more open. Opened to a new world I never knew existed. Talking to Chip was happening more often. I wasn't sure he could hear me, but I did it anyway, praying that he could.

The more I talked, the more I felt compelled to stay alive.

The madness of sadness was getting a little easier to cope with too. It was still hard not hearing his voice though. Especially since mine bounced off the walls quite often.

I missed him like crazy. When I stopped my mind from soaking up whatever it was I was reading, it never failed. The flood of tears purged forward.

I remember one particular evening very well.

While sitting on the bed, I started to unload my feelings out loud. At first, I told Chip how much I loved him, how badly I missed him, and how sorry I was for him having to experience such a horrible and tragic death. Especially the way that he died.

I told him I couldn't imagine what it must have felt like for him. How I couldn't imagine what thoughts must have roamed through his mind when it all went down.

I looked up at the ceiling and cried, "I'll never know what you went through or even what you saw, my love. I know I was with you on the phone, but I wasn't there with you in person. I wish so badly that I had been. The one thing I know for certain, my darling, is how quickly it all took place. In a matter of seconds, your life was taken from you."

I looked over at his picture sitting on the dresser and continued, "Yes, I know your body stayed alive until 5:49 a.m., but I think you immediately went into that unconscious state. You didn't hear me when I came to you."

There were times I screamed out the words, wiping away

the river of tears. My shirt became evidence of a horrid cry—it was soak and wet, and cold, rubbing against my arm. But I didn't stop there. I was determined to dig in deep.

I looked back up at the ceiling and yelled, "I can't live without you, Chip. I feel so guilty for all of this. For what happened to you. If you'd never have met me, you'd still be here. I wish we wouldn't have met. You'd be here living—breathing—the way you were meant to be. Oh, my love, I am so sorry. I swear to you—I am so sorry."

I couldn't handle any more of the torment. I crawled into bed, I pulled the covers up and over my head, I closed my eyes and before sleep took over, I whispered. "I love you, Chip Oney. Forever and ever."

I tried to get comfortable as fast as I could. I needed to pass out and escape the physical world. I needed to get away from me, quickly. Suddenly, I felt a cold chill. It surged right through me, but as fast as it appeared, it also disappeared.

"I know you're here, Chip. I love you. With all of my heart and all of my soul, I love you," I screamed.

There was another chill felt. It too surged through my body fast and then rapidly disappeared. I closed my eyes tight, when instantly I was lifted from the bed. I *knew* I was in my bed but at the same time, I felt myself being pulled upwards into the air.

I opened my eyes.

When I did, I gasped. In the blink of an eye, I was standing in front of hundreds of people. They were in rows of three. As far out as I could see, there looked to be hundreds and hundreds of people—all standing in line—waiting for something.

My feet weren't on the ground; not a solid one anyway. I wasn't floating either. I was standing in place, right in front of all of those people.

The overwhelming sense of peace soothed me. And the silence—complete and orderly, organized silence. There was a bliss of peace everywhere.

I didn't have any real thoughts at the time, but I was very curious. I knew someone was with me. I sensed their presence standing beside me.

I blurted, "Why are all of these people here?"

"These are souls waiting to pass over," the voice said.

Instantly, a lady standing in the second row jumped into my sight. She had dark black hair. Her complexion was light and she wore a colorful, flowery shirt. Her son, or who I believed to be her son, was standing directly behind her.

He was holding onto her, looking around her leg, peeking at me while possibly playing hide and seek. Every time he peeked, he smiled big. I so wanted to go to him and comfort him. The pull to go was felt, but I couldn't move. I was glued in place.

The sadness for them, for their experience, swept over me. It smothered me and I felt so, so sorry for both of them.

And then suddenly, my attention was redirected to look elsewhere, to observe my surroundings. There were no walls and I wasn't in a room of sorts. There wasn't a floor. There wasn't a ceiling. Yet everything was perfect just as it was. And beautiful.

Everything was the brightest of white I'd ever seen. There didn't seem to be anything made of solid material, but I detected a white wall of fog. Or maybe it was a white fluffy cloud—it was clearly surrounding us. The cloud was also a little translucent because I could see the brilliant blue sky undeniably in the distance.

I bounced around to look back at the people. There were so many and all of them standing in a straight line, waiting their turn. They each had an unusual look about them—a blank stare. The only one who didn't have the odd stare was the little boy. He was still peeking at me from behind his mom's leg.

Once again I felt that immense feeling of sorrow for that little boy and his mom.

In an instant flash, I was aware.

My eyes still tightly closed, I could feel my body sink slowly into the bed until I was fully physically there. I turned to look at the clock; 1:12 a.m. My birthday.

My voice pierced the air, "Wow that was different. Why'd you take me there? Is it because of that little boy?"

I waited for a sign, for a voice, for anything really. But there wasn't one. I had no time to think about it either. In no time flat—it was lights out and I was sleeping again, like a zombie.

Tap—tap—tap!

Tap—tap—tap!

Scared to death, my eyes bolted open. That's not a sound someone gets comfortable hearing; tap, tap, tap. I wasn't sure where it was originating from and if it was indeed from inside the house, that wasn't a good thing.

But it all vanished pretty quickly. In the course of the past few weeks, something else had been going on. Each morning, I was forced to wake up by a loud tapping noise inside my head. Or at least it felt that way. I couldn't tell for sure if it was in my mind or in my bedroom. Regardless of where it came from, it always tapped thirty minutes before the alarm was set to go off. I was getting better with the *fear*.

Instead of jumping out of bed, grabbing my gun, and retaliating like *GI Jane*—like I did the first few times—I stayed in place, frozen, and waited for my heart to slow.

I figured out his plan … it was time to wake up.

Chapter Seventeen

SECOND OPINION

T here had been no forward progress in the arrest of Chip's killer. But there were a few new developments. The detectives seized the murderer's car the night Chip died and it was now being processed by a Forensic team. There was a slight chance something would be located in the car positive for Chip's blood.

Sadly, days later the results came back negative. My hopes were smashed. There was still a lot of evidence needing to be tested, but it was going to take a lot more time. There was nothing anyone could do, except wait.

I was baffled beyond belief. Why that evil man thought he should be allowed to live outside as a free man, seriously confused the hell out of me. He did something unthinkable. Yet, he was allowed to roam free. I didn't get it. I couldn't figure that part out.

While the detective was telling me the not-so-good news, I received another call at the same time. It was Chip's mom. After answering, she went on to tell me that one of her neighbors, Chip's friend, had a vivid dream about him as well. I was floored. There he was again. Visiting someone else.

I was extremely excited to hear more.

I asked, "What'd she dream?"

"She dreamed she was at Chip's funeral service. She was standing close to his casket and there was a man standing next to him. This man motioned for her to come closer and she did, feeling uneasy about it. As she stood next to the casket, she watched as Chip opened his eyes and stared up at her. He was screaming, *I don't want to be here. Let me out, let me out."*

"She then said she watched him move around wildly trying like heck to get out of the casket. The man who was standing next to him, whom she thought to be his father, put his hand on Chip's shoulder and told him, 'It's okay, it's okay. Lie down, lie back down.' But Chip kept insisting that he wanted out. And then she woke up."

My feet were nailed to the sidewalk; I couldn't move. That was a little different. We had no idea what to make of it either. It was easy to suggest he didn't want to be where he was— dead. And in thinking that to be the case, it felt right to assume it wasn't his time to go. Why else would he scream out those words? *I don't want to be here.*

So I began a new search. This time for help.

Professional help. Someone who could possibly assist with not only my dreams, but with Chip too.

Last week, I stumbled across a medium who offered services for free to *victims of murder.* I emailed her. When I ran this dream past her, she suggested he didn't want his ashes to remain in the urn. That he wished for them to be spread at his favorite destinations. I understood that, but only to a degree.

I remembered a conversation we had shortly before Chip died. He told me he wanted his ashes spread out over the Gator's football field and also in Key West, where he lived as a child. But if it was so peaceful and so beautiful on the other side—like all those books I read suggested—why would his ashes even matter to him? He wouldn't care.

And if she was wrong, then why did he scream, "I don't want to be here, let me out?" I didn't know, and because I didn't know, I became very worried. And worried for Chip. I didn't want him to be sad or angry. Thinking now that he was, made my frustration intensify. I didn't know how to help him, but I knew I had to find a way.

I looked for anything pertaining to the afterlife, or mediums, or dreams, or out of body experiences. I was grateful for the information this woman gave, but also scared.

When I sent this medium an email explaining my circumstances last week, she replied within an hour, via email, and even included a reading from Chip. Quite a bit of the information seemed to fit. Some didn't go anywhere and some—was downright spooky. I imagined when I shared Chip's story, his murder, in a short format; she might have felt sorrow and possibly shock.

However, her words frightened me. I was reading comments like—look out! Watch your surroundings. Be careful. Stay away from this man. He will kill you.

I was terrified for Chip after I read another comment she made—if the spreading of his ashes isn't the case, then it's possible his soul is still earthbound. If it is, you need to find a medium to help you cross Chip over to the other side where he belongs—her words verbatim.

Gulp! That was it. I'd convinced myself right then and there I needed a second opinion. She was sweet, accommodating, and I knew she was trying hard to connect. But yikes!

I didn't search for help anymore. I hunted. Chip had to be safe...

Chapter Eighteen

ROCKY MOUNTAIN HIGH

I n November, Chip put up a doggy gate in the hallway. He didn't want the kids roaming into the back bedrooms. Last night—I had another one of those vivid dreams.

I found myself walking through the living room, toting my laundry basket in my right arm, entering that hallway that suddenly had NO gate.

At the end of the hallway is a bathroom and two bedrooms; one to the right and one to the left. The bedroom on the left is the computer room and the one on the right, my bedroom.

When I reached the end of the hallway I glanced to the left. Chip was sitting there, in the office chair. He was in front of the computer, but not facing it.

Turned sideways, the left-side of his body was facing me. His hair was neat and freshly cut and he was looking down at the desk. He didn't look happy, but he didn't look sad either.

I kept walking... into my bedroom.

When I woke up this time, I was smothered in confusion.

Why didn't I stop to talk to him? I failed to walk into the room and approach him. I never said a word. Not one word. Didn't he understand I needed to talk to him? Didn't he know it was imperative I knew he was all right?

In that world over there, all I ever saw was how alive he was. I never acknowledged or even realized he was dead.

Confused? Oh yeah. With a capital C.

The need to find help was stronger than ever. It became the priority of all priorities. I Googled every conceivable way I could imagine. It was important I now find someone to help me decipher the dreams and the possible messages. But more importantly, I needed to know if Chip was earthbound or if he was indeed on the other side.

Today was going to be the day. I could feel it somehow. In addition, something new and different, happened.

It was a cool morning in March and as I laid still in bed, waking up, I stared at the ceiling. Out of nowhere, I heard a song stream through my thoughts.

~You are my sunshine, my only sunshine. You make me happy, when skies are gray. You'll never know dear, how much I love you. Please don't take my sunshine away.~

A chill danced through my entire body. But it wasn't a chill that turned me into an iceberg. Instead, it was subtle and quite pleasant and I refused to move. Slowly, a smile crawled across my face.

"That song," sounding like I was reciting a line from *Forest Gump*. "I know that song."

Indeed, I knew it. Chip sang it to me all the time. If he didn't answer his phone with, *hello baby doll*, he was singing this song instead. I loved his surprise. I'd eagerly listen to his every word, to his funny singing voice, anticipating every verse.

I hopped out of bed and walked toward the kitchen. "Wow, am I getting a message through a song now?" I asked out loud. "Or did I make that up? Maybe somewhere in the back of my mind?"

I didn't want to put too much stock in it. So I didn't. But it did bring a smile to start my day. Yes, I could feel it. Today was going to be *the* day.

I finished my morning reports and headed right to the internet highway. The way I figured it—if I found a medium last week, I could find another this week.

Just as I typed, a website popped up. Her name was Megan M. Riley. I read her information in depth, every single page. As soon as I read where she was from, Colorado, a feeling of *she's the one* came over me.

No matter what, if Chip and I discussed anything pertaining to visiting Kansas, I always misunderstood it for Colorado. So, I decided to go out on that limb and write to her.

Before I did anything though, I walked outside for a break. It was on the way back in when I asked myself another question.

"Is she the one?"

I heard something this time, "Yes."

I didn't question the oddity of hearing the answer though. My one-track mind was on a mission. I put an email together and before I could change anything, I clicked the send button. With nothing left to do but wait, I went back a few minutes in time.

I heard "yes", didn't I? Okay, that's interesting...

In the email, I described as briefly as I could about my relationship with Chip. I wrote that he was murdered, but gave no details. I wrote about that woman's warnings from last week and asked if she could help me figure out my dreams.

And then I received another phone call.

It was Chip's mom again. She told me that another neighbor experienced a vivid dream—with Chip. I was all ears.

I asked, "What'd she say?"

"She said she was walking outside when she saw Chip across the road standing next to his truck. He called out to her using her nickname, *PT Lady*. So she walked toward him."

"When she crossed the road and approached him, he said to her loudly, three times, *Lyn knows*. And then she instantly woke up. She had this same dream three consecutive nights. The only thing he said to her each time was, *Lyn knows*."

I was speechless.

My mind was racing. What was I supposed to have known? I was searching rapidly for a clue. Anything would be good. But I got nothing.

Breaking the silence, I heard Char asking, "What do you think it is that you know, Lyn?" I had no idea. None.

My first thought—I knew he was still alive. But Char seemed to think I was holding onto something deep inside I had somehow forgotten. Something important. That was certainly a possibility, but I had no way to find out.

I decided to take a walk outside. The weather was cool, clear, and crisp. Easy breathing weather. I loved being outdoors when it was like that.

Trying hard to figure out what I possibly knew or had somehow hidden somewhere, I thought hard. And then all of a sudden, I heard music, a song—a few words.

"Rocky mountain high, Colorado."

"Hey, I know that song," I yelled. "It's by John Denver. Where in the world did that come from?"

And then it hit me like a ton of bricks.

"Oh! It's not me. That's you, Chip. You're talking to me through songs, aren't you?" I was in complete awe.

"Okay. Okay. So what are you telling me?" I looked up at the blue sky, determined to figure it out. "Colorado. She's the one isn't she? Megan. She's the one, right?"

I waited, but I didn't hear anything back.

I headed back inside and pulled up my email. There she was. With a large amount of anxiety and lots of curiosity too, I opened her response.

Her words were reassuring. She explained the bizarre job that medium's had piecing messages together and then interpreting them. She said it was possible the other lady simply misinterpreted Chip's messages.

She said the energy she was getting from Chip indicated that he was fine. He had crossed over. She said he was visiting me more often to appease my grief.

"He's not an earthbound, meaning he's not stuck," she wrote. "He doesn't give off that kind of energy. Earthbounds have a thick mucus feel to them and Chip does not have this."

I was ecstatic. Reading those words—he's not earthbound —provided a tremendous amount of relief. All of that worry exhaled right from my body. I needed to know he was safe and right then... I knew he was.

She also said it was extraordinary and unusual how he came through strong, and right away. She explained that it normally took a while to get used to how to communicate from the other side.

"I guess that speaks to the connection the two of you have," she wrote.

She also added, "Once someone starts giving warnings more than *be careful while driving* is a big red flag for truth or not. I get frustrated when I hear stories like yours and what may be well-meaning mediums communicating what is not there. On the other side, all is well and beautiful. Your life is not in danger."

She had confirmed what I believed to begin with. I wasn't in any danger. I was never so happy to have found this woman. I felt an immediate peace with her.

She also told me that dreaming is one of the easiest ways for loved ones to contact us. She assured me he was with me. She said I could have a better relationship with him now. Better than the one I had when he was here.

"True, you will never have the physical closeness that the two of you shared, but you can have access to what is the best of him now," she wrote.

The best news so far? "I will be happy to work with you and appease your fears, as well as contact Chip," she wrote.

Contact Chip?

Oh yeah, I needed to contact Chip all right. There wasn't a doubt about that. I took no time to reply. The date was set. Next Tuesday, March 18th, at 7:00 p.m.

I was positive Chip would be there…

Chapter Nineteen

THE READING

M egan asked that I relax and think about Chip for thirty minutes before the reading. So I went outside to sit. I drank in the fresh crisp air. I looked up into the clear blue sky and then closed my eyes tightly. After taking in several deep breaths and holding them in before exhaling, my heartbeat slowed. I was relaxed.

When I opened my eyes, I watched a beautiful monarch butterfly fluttering about. I was mesmerized. I followed it everywhere it went as it flew over the back yard, up the side of the house, into the trees, and then up and over the roof. I sensed Chip's presence and knew he was there.

At seven o'clock on the nose my phone rang; I was speaking with Megan. Her voice was delicate, soft, and unique. Once the introductions were over she asked me if I had any specific questions I wanted to ask Chip.

"No. I didn't think of that," I said. "I've never contacted anyone before. I'm basically here for the ride, so to speak." We both laughed.

"Okay. Well, let's begin."

There was a brief silence before she started.

Megan: Eyes. What I see mostly are eyes. A two-sided sweetness. His sadness is for you and everything that you've gone through. I see a teddy bear, a brown stuffed teddy bear. Does the teddy bear make sense to you?

Lyn: I wrote him a letter recently and in it, I said he
        was my teddy bear. That was after he died
        though.

Megan: Okay. It's like he's showing me a circus. Did
        you ever go to the circus together?

Lyn: No, we never went to a circus.

Megan: He's such a goofball. He's lunging in front of
        me as if to say he has no pain. He feels good. No
        pain. He's on top of a circus ball bouncing all
        over the place. He feels so good.
        Now he's saying not everyone saw him the way
        that you did. He appears gruff. He's a big man.
        He was unhappy with his appearance. He shows
        himself in front of a mirror. Was he unhappy
        with his appearance?

Lyn: Yes, he was. I always said he was a big man, but
        not a heavy man. He was handsome to me.

Megan: Yeah, he wasn't happy about his appearance.
        About his passing. I know that I know some
        things, but we're still going to go there.
        There is an impact. He feels like he's here, but
        not here. Much confusion. It doesn't make sense
        to him. Pain is being shown to me on the top of
        his head.
        Okay, his physicalness—he has chosen an
        outline of his body, just as he was when he
        passed, just as you know him. He did not choose to
        go back to when he was younger or to when he
        looked younger.
        Oh, I have to share this with you. I found a letter
        I wrote. It began with, *Dear Chip; thank you so
        much for coming to me*. Normally, I send out

thank you letters to clients after we've had a reading together. I found this letter already written, before our communications, before this reading. Isn't that neat?

Lyn: Yes. Yes, it is.

She reflected such excitement about the note but I wasn't in the same place. I couldn't fathom why she would write to Chip before I even contacted her?

Megan: The look he gives you is like basking in the moonlight. Oh how he adores you. He's giving you a sense of reassurance like *if I were right there, I would hug you.* He is okay. He is so happy.
Did he have awkwardness in his knees or have joint pain? He's showing me pain in his knees.

Lyn: Yes, he did have pain in his knees. But he never complained about his pain.

Megan: He says, "Nothing hurts." He says, "I can do it all." He's out seeing things. He travels a lot. Did the two of you plan on building a house or plan to buy a new house?

Lyn: Yes. We've been searching for our own house for a long time.

Megan: Well, he's building you a house. He's waiting for you. He has lots to do and it's like no time passes. He's waiting for you, however long it is.

Lyn: Can I ask how long that will be?

Megan: We all have free will, but I do see you here for decades and decades and decades. His sadness is in your sadness. All of those times, he's right there next to you. Especially when you're half-awake to connect.

Lyn: Did he know what was happening to him that
          morning when he was shot?

Megan: Right before, yes, he knew. He shows me two
          men facing the same way—execution like—he
          did know. And you know the person too.

There's no way she could have known that—me knowing the
person. I didn't share that with her. And it wasn't in the news
either. I was amazed. Wow!

Lyn: Is it the same person the police believe too?

Megan: Yes.

Lyn: Does he want us, his mom and I, to keep
          searching for clues in the investigation?

Megan: He doesn't care. He's turning around and
          looking away, like it doesn't matter to him. No,
          your focus is to be somewhere else. "Don't
          focus on the murder," he says. He's showing me
          a shed that leans to a pool house. Under
          blankets, like the ones moving companies use,
          quilted. It's (the gun) under things like that.
          He's saying, "Both of you grieve so I can't be
          around you more. Once your sadness is
          tunneled, then there's more contact with you.
          Go deep; there is more of me than the sadness.
          After you feel more relief, there's much more
          contact possible."

Lyn: So what you're saying is when our grief
          subsides, our contact will be more?

Megan: Yes, that's right. He is waiting for you. For a
          long time he will be waiting for you. Again, it
          will be decades.
          Now he's taking your face in his hands and
          smothering you with kisses. He kisses you

everywhere; on your nose, on your head, your
eyes, your lips, everywhere. He loves you very
much.

Lyn: I love him very much.

There was a pause, so I decided to slip in a question.

Lyn: Is there anything he'd like for me to share with
his mom?

Megan: I see him lunging again. He says, "I am so good.
Look at me, I can do anything. No pain, mom."
I see purple flowers. He loves these flowers.
There's a purple connection.
Now he's dressed in a grass skirt. He's shaking
it all around. He's such a goofball.

Lyn: Are you sure it's a grass skirt? Or is it a skirt of
some kind?

Megan: No, it's a grass skirt and he's wearing a coconut
bra. Did you guys go to Hawaii?

Lyn: I've gone twice, but he didn't go with me.

I asked him to go with me both times. Instead, we hung out
on the phone. So in one respect, he did accompany me...just
not in person. My sister was so upset with me...I spent more
time with Chip on the phone than I did with her and my
nephew.

Megan: He's shaking the skirt all around. He's so funny.
He says, "I love you. I miss you, I'm here. I'm
always around you, for both of you."
Okay, now I see a Dutch oven. Did he ever pull
the covers over your head after he farted? He's
laughing so hard.

Lyn: Yes, he did. He did that one time and one time
only. And yes, he laughed so hard I thought he

was going to fall out of the bed.

I couldn't believe Chip mentioned that. It happened the weekend before he was murdered. We were watching TV in bed when I heard him pass gas. The next thing I saw were the covers coming up and over my head.

"Whew that was a bad one. Take a whiff, darlin'," he said, through his obnoxious laughter.

We wrestled and I tried diligently to get out but I couldn't. I was laughing too hard. He won. Of course. It truly was a funny moment. One I won't forget.

Megan: Okay, going to the beach. You're walking on the beach. The rocks are bigger and the sand hurts your feet. Then you'll walk on softer sand and he's walking with you. There are pebbles in the sand and you'll look down and something star-like will be from him. Not a starfish, but something star-like.

Lyn: Okay, thank you.
       What kind of house is he building?

Megan: It has wood planks inside, big grain but not cedar. It's a boardwalk house. It has a large walkway, big windows, a huge plant—it's a shorter palm tree, but its huge sitting directly in the middle of the house. It has a big outdoor living room, an outdoor kitchen; the perfect temperature all around. There's openness about it. The cross breeze is wonderful. It has a look of cutting curtains flowing in the breeze. It's a log cabin, but the grain is darker.

We wanted a log cabin home. There's no way she could have known. We talked about it all the time. Dreaming it up in

132

our minds, hoping we'd find one in Jacksonville.

Megan: Now he's swapping bubblegum with you. Did the two of you ever swap bubblegum?

Lyn: Yes, we did.

Megan: He's showing me that the two of you swapped bubblegum. How sweet.

This was interesting. She couldn't have known we swapped gum. One afternoon we were heading out and I was chewing my last piece and he asked if I had another one. I didn't. So I pulled the gum from my mouth and put it in front of his lips.

He laughed and then opened wide and wrapped his lips over my fingers, gently kissing them. I knew he was happy.

Megan: He has much work to do. When you want to talk, he's here. It's like he shows me that he can be in more than one place at a time. At the circus again, there are three rings and he can be in all of them at the same time.

Lyn: He said he was confused when he passed over?

Megan: He shows dizziness—like not knowing your bearings. As in the movie *Ghost*, there's a light that shines out of nowhere and a figure is at the end. Someone small who's there waiting for him to cross. A small male, and they hold hands and walk across together. That moment is so beautiful for him and so horrible for you. He only had a few minutes of confusion. Did he have a brother who passed?

Lyn: No, I don't think so. His only brother is still alive.

Megan: He shows me a book; he's in school. He travels a lot. He's out flying, seeing things. He's like

the cartoon character *Underdog* flying over the
water looking at cruise ships and going out as
far as he can go to places he's never been
before. He's taking in a lot.

Now he's showing me a flower. He's saying,
"You saw the best in me. I'm here, I can be
here, be in contact."

Lyn: Is he here with me, or is he there with you?

Megan: I think he takes turns between the two of us.
You should take pictures. Ask for him to be
there and take pictures of your surroundings.
You can catch your loved one in photos. There
have been amazing pictures taken with orbs in
them.

Lyn: That's a great idea. Has he quieted down now?

Megan: Yes, a little bit. Would you like to go over the
dreams?

Lyn: Yes, please.

We then went over a few dreams I had documented.

Dream: *The one where we went to the car dealership
requesting new rug mats. He said, 350 and I
said, 349.*

Megan: *This is a time, not a gun.*

Dream: *The dream when Chip said, I'm okay, but you
didn't have to leave your number.*

Megan: *He knows where to find you.*

Dream: *The same night when we were hovering above
the ground with a song, the metal object, and
the ocean.*

Megan: *Chip is showing you things that he can.*

Dream: *The morning I woke up with 4:45*

pounding in my head and I questioned if this
was when he was shot.

Megan: Yes, 4:45 is the time.

Dream: The dream when I watched a ball of energy
come over my bed and enter my chest.

Megan: This was him moving into you.

Dream: The dream about seeing lots of people in three
rows. When the voice said, "These are souls
waiting to cross."

Megan: These are people passing right now. Groups of
them. And a lot of them are children. Young men
saying, "I'm done, I'm out of here." There are
shifts, 20/12 shifts. They are assisting us; there
are many rainbow children.

Our call ended and I sat the phone down quietly on the desk.
For a moment I stared at it, but then the overwhelming
emotions of guilt, sadness, grief, and the unrelenting yearning
for his presence all gushed out. I cried, hard.

I swore I felt like a faucet turned on with the flood of water
escaping my eyes. Sadly, each day that had passed, the
realization was growing stronger… he was never coming
home.

An hour or so went by and the incredibly horrid emotions
calmed. I reflected back. Did any of it make sense? Did Chip
give her messages to relay?

The Hawaii connection was remarkable. I could see him
dancing in a grass skirt. He was a funny guy and he loved to
make me laugh. When she called him a goofball, I thought that
was quite interesting too. His nickname was *Goofball*.

After she mentioned the bubblegum swapping, I knew she
was connected. I didn't think anything of it when it happened,
the bubblegum swap, so I was surprised it came up. Maybe he

used it as a way to show me it was him.

The Dutch oven message—what a trip. That was a first for me and I have to say, Chip shocked the heck out of me.

All three of those communications were directly related to *us*. They were personal and nothing Megan could have known. Did she connect with Chip? Absolutely, she did.

Did Chip give me what I needed? Without a shadow of a doubt, he certainly tried. Sadly, he no longer had the power to give me what I needed.

The only thing I needed … was the physical *him*.

Chapter Twenty

MEETING IN THE MIND

A s I tried to convince myself I was making stuff up, I tried even harder to persuade myself to believe in the events unfolding. I was still lost, but trying desperately to be found.

I loved the feeling from learning new things about the other side. It seemed the more I dug in, the more I received. It was amazing but at the same time, bizarre and confusing.

For example: I walked outside one afternoon to pace. I was minding my own business, thinking to myself, when I heard clearly—out of nowhere—*I'll stand by you.*

I jumped clean out of my skin. I heard her voice, Carrie Underwood's voice, sing those few words. I looked for a witness to the interruption but no one was near. So I went back to the song.

How powerful those few words. I'll stand by you—a solid message stating that he'll never leave and will always stand by me. I knew I wasn't making it up, but darn it was hard to accept that something was roaming around in my head I had no control over.

Another example—bizarre but beautiful:

I was blessed to have the job I had. As long as I had my work completed, I was allowed the freedom to roam. I did a lot of walking at work. And a lot of thinking.

I tried hard *not* to reflect back to *that* ugly morning. Instead, I forced myself to remember particular conversations we had. Or remember the mini-vacations we shared, or remember our one-on-one moments together. Anything other than that horrible morning.

I wanted to celebrate an anniversary, so I tried to remember the actual day we met. I couldn't remember the date. I tried to remember the night we first kissed, but I couldn't remember that either. Frustrated, I then tried to think of any day that was special for us—but I couldn't remember any of them.

The devastated tears sped across my face as I stared up into the blue sky and cried out.

"We don't even have an anniversary, Chip!"

The sorrow poured whilst the battle continued. I wanted to remember one, only one, special date. And then out of nowhere, a voice was heard. There was no mistaking it. It was lucid, concise, and straight to the point.

"Every day is our anniversary."

It was so clear and so forceful, I couldn't ignore it.

I was stunned. As quickly as those tears began, they were turned off. At the same time I swore I felt something dash right through me. It was comparable to an energy boost of some kind. I was feeling good and nothing seemed to matter. Literally, I was on top of happy.

Every day was our anniversary. We weren't celebrating our love one day out of the year; we were celebrating it every day. I truly wanted to believe this. So… I did.

I was starting to look forward to the weekends again.

More than I did before Chip died. It was the only time I had for me. A time when I didn't have to worry about getting anything done. I could cry if I wanted to, and I did, or I could try to move about and accomplish a task or two.

On one particular weekend, I took a ride to *Michael's Arts and Craft Store.* We had purchased a few posters in the Florida Keys for our new home and I wanted to see about getting them framed.

I was picking out the frames, alone, wondering why I was even there. Deep down, I knew it though. The visual reminders of our memories were still needed. Chip's love, was still wanted.

The horrible urge to cry required every ounce of strength I had to fight it off. Surprisingly, I succeeded and exited the store as quickly as I could. The immense sadness was on the verge of detonating. And then—someone shouted at me.

"Why you look so sad? I'll stand by you."

I stopped—right there in the middle of the parking lot. I looked all around; beside me, behind me, back at the store. I searched for anyone close by... there wasn't a person near.

I wasn't looking for the one who said it, not really. Instead, I was looking for someone who also *heard* it.

That voice was that loud.

It shocked me, knocked me off my feet. I hurried to the car. I couldn't help it, I crashed. The fact that he was dead and I was alive—it was devastatingly sad.

I screamed at him, "How can you think I'm not supposed to be sad? Are you flippin' nuts?"

How could Chip think I shouldn't be sad? That upset me.

Driving in the state I was in wasn't a good idea. So I stood outside the car waiting for the flood to subside. When I was better, I drove home. And then that's when it hit me. That's when I put two and two together.

"Hey, he talked to me again."

Yes, Chip was talking to me. It may have been by way of a song, but it didn't matter. Chip had found a way to talk to me.

"How neat is that?" I said, out loud.

I was feeling much better.

I took the kids outside to run around. The weather was great that time of year. A few minutes later, I found myself sitting on the steps, zoned out, all thoughts removed, when I heard someone scream from behind.

"Jeremiah was a bullfrog."

I leaped up, turned around, and searched for the person that vocalized that. Whoever it was had scared me to death. That voice was extremely loud.

But there wasn't anyone in my back yard.

That's when I realized—I wasn't experiencing the voices on the outside in my physical world, they were actually coming from within. Inside my mind. And they were very distracting.

I laughed out loud. That song, it threw me into the past and reminded me of a very special moment Chip and I had shared shortly before he was murdered. A moment where we screamed at the top of our lungs, singing this very song on our way home from grocery shopping.

I smiled. Especially when I remembered the continued words—*joy to the world, joy to you and me.*

It didn't matter if there was a message. I didn't care.

Chip was still here ... just in a different way.

Chapter Twenty-One

I AM YOUR HUSBAND

C hip was communicating and I got it—he was still alive. Okay, maybe not alive in the sense of his physical body, but I knew he was real.

Picturing what it was like on the other side was a major struggle. What I couldn't wrap my head around—was what he looked like now, today. Was he that little ball of energy? Or was he instead a thought-based ideal.

As much as Chip's communications excited me and as much as his new life was an even stronger belief system...it didn't seem to change the fact that he wasn't alive in his physical body. The hole in my heart remained wide open and very raw.

The bouncing back and forth from believing he still existed to not believing, I reeled like a yo-yo. One afternoon I fell into a deep, queasy, mood wondering if I needed to turn away and leave everything behind. Put this afterlife stuff and Chip deep into the past.

I was pacing back and forth the length of the sidewalk when I professed out loud, "Why aren't I giving up and trying to let you go? You're dead, Chip. Dead! This isn't how it's supposed to be done."

I was at that point. Grief was winning out that day.

At that very moment, I heard a voice I absolutely recognized. She was singing—sharing four little words.

"I honestly love you."

It was Olivia Newton-John's voice streaming through my head. My knees buckled. I fell to the ground. I didn't ask where that had come from. Instead, I looked up and stared hard into the sky. I had to do it; I had to repeat his words.

"I honestly love you, too, my love."

I was in love with a dead man.

A dead man who was communicating. It was a beautiful moment and it left me speechless. I sat for a long time staring up into the empty sky. My heart aching for him.

I didn't know it then, but that was a defining moment. One that would help drive me forward into a new journey. Talking to my dead fiancé wasn't only normal, it was about to become my life. My new life.

After regaining my composure, I stood up and shook off the sadness. A couple of minutes later and a few steps forward, I was knocked over again with a new song. I recognized the artist—*The Beatles.* They were singing, but only shared seven words.

"Eight days a week, I love you."

"I think he knows I can hear the songs now," I whispered.

It was so like him to try and make me laugh when I was down. I think he knew that as much as his communications thrilled me, shaking the grief was very hard. No matter what I did, what I read, what I focused on, I ultimately cried for hours on end. Sometimes so badly that I had to stop and look at myself in the mirror. That person staring back was a complete stranger.

I worried why everything he did wasn't good enough. I should be happy, not sad. So I escaped as much as I could.

By sleeping.

If I was going to save me, I had to *escape* me.

Sometimes I slept with no recollection of dreams and other times, I bounced awake marveling at the experience.

On this particular day, I chose to sleep.

And then, I slowly opened my eyes.

Far, far away, walking across a very large grassy knoll, Chip was heading my way. He was waving, excitedly. A beam of delight suddenly rushed through me and the joy and anticipation of seeing him welled up inside. I couldn't wait to hug him and kiss him.

I suddenly noticed how dark it was.

The sun was dimly lit in the background shedding colors of bright yellows, dark oranges, and black, all illuminating the sky behind Chip.

"Is it sunset or is it sunrise?" I couldn't be sure.

Because of the dark, it was difficult to make out what he was wearing. He was a silhouette, waving. He seemed far away yet looked so close at the same time. And his walk—I noticed his stride instantly.

I also noticed someone else. Chip was holding a little boy's hand. The boy was short, a little over half the size of Chip. He was a child, or a young person; it was unclear because he, too, was a silhouette. And like Chip, he too was waving enthusiastically.

"Awe, isn't he the cutest," I gushed with pride.

I couldn't wait to meet the boy and see him up close.

I stood still, waiting. They weren't in a very big rush, strolling slowly. So I turned to look at the rolling hills.

The sun had set a bit more and the green was no longer. But the majestic beauty sat in place longing for attention. The rolling hills were seen as far out in the distance as the eyes would allow. It literally took my breath away—it was so beautiful there. What surprised me most was the energy I felt when I breathed it all in. It took me to a happier place, one where I hadn't been before.

I turned back to see where the guys were—half way now. They were still walking over the large hill and still waving, passionately. I waved back and hollered, "Hurry up," and then I laughed.

Their happiness was floating across the field; I felt it crash inside of me. My every thought was taken away. Our reunion was certainly going to be a beautiful one... if they'd only hurry.

My alarm clock screamed loudly and my eyes shot open—I was wide awake.

"That was a dream? Damn, it felt real," I howled out.

I didn't get the chance to meet the little guy nor give Chip a big hug, and that saddened me. But at the same time, I was in complete awe. I'd never seen anything so darn exquisite.

I wondered if the boy was the one who helped Chip cross over. It certainly felt like it, but I didn't get the chance to see him up close or ask if he was Chip's brother.

I hadn't yet figured out *how* to communicate. I was opening up, little by little, even I could see that. However, I didn't realize that the easiest way to communicate was to be still and to listen. I would get there, but it would take more time.

Because of my exploring ways, I knew our connection was getting stronger. And much quicker. There wasn't a day between the communications allowed now. Instead, it was every day and only hours apart. If he wasn't earthbound—I knew he wasn't—he certainly seemed to be.

After seeing him and the little boy, I hopped out of bed and headed to the kitchen for coffee. Instead of walking through the living room like normal, I decided to go through the dining room.

As I walked through the thickly framed entrance-way, I

experienced an overwhelming sensation. It was warm, a feel good feeling, like an *in love* emotion and it swooped down and vibrated my entire body, embracing me.

I felt a hint of dizziness, so I stopped in place when instantaneously, I heard a voice.

"I am your husband."

I was stunned. Not so much about the message but more about how it appeared. The love was amazing and it felt incredible; I never felt so adored.

My sweetheart was doing everything he could to make me understand he was alive, real, not a figment of imagination playing games with me. He loved me like no one ever loved me before.

A veil of indescribable love was greeting me each day ... the shield of sadness was no longer desired.

Chapter Twenty-Two

REACH OUT

I nterpreting my dreams was much harder than I thought. As much as I wanted to be able to figure them out myself, looking at them in a literal sense wasn't revealing the entire scope of their messages.

So one afternoon I decided to reach out to Megan. She had helped me understand that Chip wasn't earthbound and that his communications were out of our love for each other. I was hoping she'd be able to help me decipher more, so I was excited when she answered my call.

I started our conversation, "I had another one of those vivid dreams with Chip, but this one was a little disturbing. The dream was a two day episode. On the first day, he told me he was going back into the service and would be gone for two years. He said he wanted me to go on living, without him. On the second day, I searched everywhere trying to find him, but he was already gone."

"When I woke up, Megan, I knew I had to call him, immediately, and tell him that our relationship was more important than letting it go. I wanted to tell him we would figure something out."

"Do you think he was trying to tell me to move on?"

Megan answered, "You are so psychic. You didn't know that before all of this, did you?"

I replied, "No. I can't say I did. Being psychic has never crossed my mind, not even once."

She continued, "I don't feel he feels you're in a place to move on. There will be a time, years down the road, when you will, but now is not the time to worry about that. How I see it is—a relationship will naturally develop. He will know and understand the connection you will always have with Chip. I feel it's more now that you know your relationship with Chip is stronger and more important than death. That you figured something out, that's pretty profound. It usually takes people a long time to come to that."

I almost cried, "Profound? It all feels more like determination. Not just from my side of things, but from his as well. I still feel him. And my sadness gets less and less, but it's only because I understand he's still here with me. Does that make sense?"

"Going from never paying much attention to what I call woo-woo stuff, to reading as much as you have and getting messages, dreams, and mediumship communication, it is a positive reflection of your connection and your commitment to each other. Figuring something out is something you have spoken of many times. That you would dream about it is only normal."

"But when I was inside the dream, Megan, I didn't know it *was* a dream. It felt so real. And two years has come up so many times. Something's going to happen in two years. I can feel it. This is where I get lost in figuring out the dream-visits."

"I don't think you're imagining the two," she said. "Two is a number about truth, peace, loyalty, and love. How does it feel if when you see or hear the two, it's a signal that you're on the right track? It could also be that in two years is when you feel ready to move on."

I acknowledged the number two and then allowed her comment to sit for a minute. It made sense. And then I changed the subject, like I always do.

"Something happened the other day that freaked me out. One evening, I changed into my pajama pants and then walked toward the bathroom. As I passed through the doorway, I saw my pajama's covered in blood. The waistband, down to my knees, was nothing but red. I stood there for a minute in a daze wondering what the heck happened. I didn't feel any fear or pain, but it was a very clear image. Later, I wondered if I might get raped or violently hurt. Or I might pass from a bad female problem that caused the bleeding. What do you think?"

"It's interesting you saw this blood in the threshold of a door," she stated. "If you look at thresholds, you can sometimes see spirit. I don't get a warning or a threat to you; however, I did see a flash about reproductive organs. Always taking into account free-will, predicting a death isn't something I do much of, but will give gentle *be careful when driving* precautions if I see something."

"Ultimately, it's up to you, your body, and soul when you'll cross and only you can answer that. I saw that you would be here for a while, and that you and Chip would be re-united, seeming like no time had passed. Did we talk about angels? I keep getting angels. Doreen Virtue's books and this author I discovered, Joyce Keller, *Calling All Angels*. It might be beneficial for you to learn and feel yours and Chip's angels, as well as the ascended masters."

I wrote the titles down and thanked her for her help. Then I remembered something amazing I wanted to share.

"I have two incredible validations that came out of our visit last week. One, Hawaii—I've been twice. Before our phone visit, I had rearranged a few magnets on the refrigerator. Pictures of Chip are plastered all over it. The magnet I replaced and put on top of his picture was one I purchased in Hawaii. It's made of wood and has four flowers with *Hawaii* engraved on it."

"The other day I turned to look at his picture when out of the blue it hit me. I could have sworn someone slapped me across the face because there it was. The Hawaii magnet—right on top of him. I have no clue why I didn't see that earlier, I just smiled. Could this be what he was talking about? He's here, yet he's not here?"

She squealed, "That gives me chills. I love hearing that stuff. Most of the time I get the picture and not a lot of reference to it. Hawaii, with his picture under the magnet, left for you to recognize, is perfect. Feels like undeniable proof he's saying, *I'm here, I see you, I'm with you.*"

After describing the dream-visit with Chip and the little boy shown in silhouette, I asked Megan, "Do you think this could have been the boy who helped Chip cross?"

She answered, "It could be. He was there to meet Chip and take him over. Sweet little boy, or small man. He seemed young. I wonder if his mother lost a brother or a son?"

Chapter Twenty-Three

ENDLESS POSSIBILITIES

H is mom told me she didn't have a brother who passed young. However, she did tell me she had a miscarriage in the span of time between Chip and his younger brother.

There wasn't any proof, but everything was leaning in that direction. The younger boy beside Chip, in that dream, he had to be his brother.

Before Megan and I hung up, I set up a time to chat again. Talking things out with her uplifted me. It gave me a new confidence and one I hadn't felt in a long time.

I wasn't kidding... I had no one to turn to. No one to talk to. Chip was my best friend. In a lot of respects, he was my only friend. Megan was this outsider able to look inside. She became my window to the afterlife. Even if I didn't realize it then—she was my window.

"You're going to laugh," I told her. "Last week you said Chip was like the cartoon character *Underdog* flying around traveling, seeing things he hasn't seen before, remember?"

"Yes..."

"Well this morning, I traveled a different way to work. On the side of the road, a wrecker was facing me, parked, broken down. In big and bold letters, I saw *Underdog* plastered on the front of the hood. I had to laugh, Megan. I've lived here for twenty-five years and have never seen that wrecker service before. Pretty neat, right?"

"I love that," she said with a boisterous laugh. "He's been

sending you extra hints and hellos. I wonder what's next."

"Ha! I was thinking the same thing; what's next? Do you think it's possible he can move a rearview mirror? Yesterday when I hopped in the car, my mirror was completely shifted to one side—in the opposite direction. I hadn't touched it, in months. So, I wondered if he could… you know… do that?"

"It takes a lot of energy to move things on this side. But I wouldn't be surprised. I kept seeing car keys moved. That's why I mentioned that. Car—keys—mirror, I can get that."

"Oh that's right. You did tell me he was messing with my keys. How'd I forget that?"

"My grandmother turns lights off and one time apport an earring—meaning I didn't have this earring before. She sent it over from the other side. Cool, huh?"

"Are you serious? How can they do something like that?"

Her grandmother apport an earring? Is she for real? Wow. Just believe, Lyn. No matter what you hear or what you see, keep believing. There are tons of ways to communicate. You've only experienced a drop in the ocean.

"I have no idea how they do it," she said. "I've read other accounts where they've brought over flowers, pictures, jewelry, etc. Apparently the items disappear after a while. Maybe the energy it holds we don't need any longer, I'm not sure. If I ask about the mirror, I see him with a goofy grin. So I'm feeling yes, it was him moving your rearview mirror."

I knew he moved that mirror, wow. How exciting!

"I received an email from that first medium I told you about. She wrote something that caught my eye today. She said, 'We are all bonded together by love. We've always been that way, even in our past lives together.' Do you believe that? If it's true, about past lives, it would mean Chip and I have known each other before this life."

"I haven't shared this before now," I continued. "In December, Chip and I realized we had met once before. We were in our teens at the same Navy base one summer in Orlando, Florida. He was living with his dad, and my sister and I were staying with family. We were shocked. Can it be possible we knew each other in another life?"

"I do see the two of you with a couple of lifetimes together. You have been through a lot with each other and felt you might mix it up this time. Do you remember the movie *Made in Heaven* from the eighties? I think it was Kelly Preston and Timothy Hutton who starred in it. That's who the two of you remind me of. Especially with being at the same time in the same place."

"I never thought of it like that—same time, same place," I said, dazed. "I'll have to go and find that movie now. Do you think he's around me because I want him to be? Or is it because he wants to be? Or is it both?"

"I feel he's around for both of you. He is because he wants to and he can. He can also be doing his work at the same time. He's also around because you're asking for him. The comment that other medium made and implied—they have the same time/space limitations there as we have here, is poppycock. There is no death, just the removal of the physical apparatus."

"Your head will probably still try to figure this out," she explained, "There isn't a real way to wrap your mind around everything."

"I get that," I responded. "Do you think I'm communicating with Chip? I do believe we're connected, but sometimes I feel like I'm crazy. And it's doubly-hard because I can't talk to anyone about these dreams I have."

"As long as you think you're crazy, you're good," she said.

"When you don't think that anymore, is when to be concerned. I do think you've connected with him. The problem is our conditioning that this kind of communication isn't possible. It is possible, and you have many examples of it that aren't by accident, or a coincidence. I ask myself how it feels. If the exchange or interaction feels good, then it's real. If it feels strange or uncomfortable, then it's probably my mind."

"A teacher told me this once, it might help. 'Yes, you could be making it up, but of all the thoughts you could have had, why do you think you had that one?' You know in your heart what's true and real. Find people you can talk to. When you speak it, the message becomes more real."

When you speak it, it becomes more real. What powerful words. And look, goose bumps all across my arm. I do share, a little. With my sister mostly and a little with Chip's mom too. Neither of them think I'm going insane. I couldn't help but remember the time a co-worker said, "How do you ever sleep? I'm worried about you."

That's when I got worried. She caused me to shut down. The risk was too great—I didn't want to be committed to an institution for talking to my dead lover.

"How the heck can you check in and get a message, Megan? That's what I want to do. I want to get the pictures so I can see what he's saying," I told her.

"It's hard to explain. I've always had a gift and enhanced the Clairs with hard work. While quieting down this side, I'm able to hear, see, taste, and smell what's on the other side. Chip's energy seems to have calmed down since we first connected. He's still a goofball and continues with the circus thing, but isn't as insistent as when I first felt him."

"Ha!" I said with a laugh. "It's so funny to hear you call him a goofball. I always called him a darn goofball. And yes, I have to agree, he has calmed down a little bit. Most of what I'm getting this week is while I'm awake. The thoughts, the rearview mirror moving, the tickles, the songs, etc. I love these too. It makes him all that more real."

"You know, I was thinking," I had another reflection, "Since his death, I've done nothing but try to search for ways to communicate with him. I think it was about the third week after he died when I went to an event by *Sylvia Browne*. My key—oh my God! That just slapped me in the face, Megan—my key to the car was in his sweat shirt that I wore that night. And twice it fell out. He was messing with my keys! I can't believe I missed that. I wore it all day and not once, did anything fall out. But that evening, that key bounced out twice and each time, hit the floor."

"Keys!" she shouted. "I'm telling you he's been messing with your keys. I'm so glad you remembered that. That's the neat thing about medium readings. What doesn't make sense at the time of the reading hits later, like little gifts. So cool. I love this stuff."

I was loving it, too. When I heard from him, no matter the way, I soared high into the heavens with joy. Everything was still about him. It was still about us.

Sometimes I had this overwhelming emotion telling me I could do this. As long as I believed—believed he was still with me—I knew I could do this—live with him being there in that afterlife.

My life was still him and about continuing our relationship. It sounded strange; I knew that... to suggest a relationship past physical death. But it was all I had left. How could I deny him? I couldn't. I had to believe.

"What's hard to understand is what's truly out there," I projected. "Remember the visit when that melon-sized energy ball entered my chest—in that dream I swear I was awake but I can't be sure. Could Chip have left something behind? The reason I ask is because I have these little vibrations running through me I haven't had before. And whenever I think of him or I start talking to him, I get these goose bumps even when it's eighty degrees outside. It baffles me."

I drifted a little off subject, "I can't describe the connection or that feeling when we were together. It was as though no one existed, except the two of us—if that makes sense."

"I feel Chip knows that you know he's around, and that you don't question the awake things as much anymore. So he doesn't have to come at night," Megan said. "I don't think he left anything behind, or that you're keeping him here or anything like that. He is around, he only left his body and will always be with you. He sees what's happening now. And while your grief isn't gone, you can feel that your relationship and love will continue."

"When I'm meditating to prepare for a client, or to clear for the day, I always get goose bumps with the voice of my guide in my head, *I am here*. It's a beautiful and reassuring thing and my way of knowing they're with me. Of course it's not eighty degrees here, but being cold and feeling spirit are two different feelings for me. I suspect it's similar for you."

"And I totally understand the world falling away when the two of you found each other and spent time together. I would recommend that movie *Made in Heaven*. It focuses on the eternity aspect of love. Love never dies, it just transforms."

Another set of powerful words, *love never dies... it just transforms*. Our world had fallen apart, yet I felt Chip's love everywhere. He had to be watching over me. What other reason could there be for all the signs, messages, and dreams? He was watching everything I did. Listening to my every thought.

Knowing exactly what I'd do and how I'd react.

Chip knows everything ... and I know nothing.

I later started questioning something Megan had said, *I've always had a gift and enhanced the Clairs with hard work.* Knowing absolutely nothing about mediumship or psychic abilities, I had no idea what she meant about *Clairs.* So I looked the word up. Much to my surprise, there was more than one.

Clairs are defined as follows:

Clairvoyance (seeing). The term clairvoyance is used to refer to the ability to gain information about an object, person, location or physical event through means other than the known human senses. A person said to have this ability is referred to as a clairvoyant ("one who sees clearly").

Clairsentience (feeling/touching). A form of extra-sensory perception when a person acquires psychic knowledge primarily by feeling. In addition, the term refers to a person who can feel the vibration of other people. There are many different degrees of clairsentience ranging from the perception of diseases to the thoughts or emotions of other people. This kind of ability cannot have a vivid picture in the mind. Instead, a very vivid feeling can form.

Clairalience (smelling). Also known as clairescent, this person accesses psychic knowledge through the physical sense of smell.

Clairgustance (tasting). Those who possess this ability are able to perceive the essence of a substance from the spiritual or ethereal realms through taste. This Clair allows one to taste a substance without putting anything in one's mouth.

Claircognizance (knowing). This person has the ability to acquire psychic information primarily by means of intrinsic knowledge. It is the ability to know something without a physical explanation why one knows it; like the concept of mediums.

Clairaudience (hearing/listening). This ability refers to the actual perception of sounds such as voices, tones, or noises which are not apparent to other humans or to recording equipment. For instance, a clairaudient person might claim to hear the voices or thoughts of the spirits of persons who are deceased.

Clairtangency (clear touching). This Clair is more commonly known as psychometry. It is the ability to handle an object and perceive Psychic information from the spiritual or ethereal realms using touch.

Clairempathy (clear emotion). Someone with this ability tunes into the vibrations of the spiritual and ethereal realms and feels the tones of another's aura. It is the ability to Psychically tune into others emotions.

Chapter Twenty-Four

TILL THE END OF TIME

T here was a surprise in store for me the last Saturday of March. Scooby needed a bath, badly. He had grown so fast that I never imagined I'd be unable to bathe him myself. My back had gotten worse and couldn't stand up to the task.

I set my alarm the night before to get up early. When I heard a man rambling on the radio, I reached over to hit the snooze button. I'm the biggest snoozer ever. I've never been one to hop out of bed on the first try.

Five minutes later the radio blared again, this time with a song. As soon as I heard the first words, *No One*, I felt a charge of electricity shoot straight through my body.

I was flat on my back, unable to move, shaking. It wasn't a painful feeling. Instead, it felt like an electrical vibration. If I imagined myself plugged into a socket somehow, I would quickly become its hostage while experiencing the lowest possible energy current it was capable of delivering.

All of my attention was so focused on that charging vibration, I had failed to pay attention to the radio until halfway through the song. When I knew I wasn't in trouble, I heard her voice singing loudly.

~I know some people search the world to find something like what we have. I know people will try, try to divide something so real. So till the end of time, I'm telling you, there ain't no one.~

I was sucked in hard. I listened intently to every single word and as soon as it was over, the constant vibration was as well. It just stopped. I sat straight up, shook my head, and then said, "I think I was supposed to pay attention to that song."

It was evident I was meant to hear it.

I went through my morning routine, took Scooby to the bath shop, and then called my sister.

"Who sings this song?" I asked her. I sang a few words that I could remember and then out of nowhere, she was singing them too. "Alicia Keys," she laughed.

No way! Keys? Seriously?

I sat for a moment with my mouth hanging wide open.

"Are you sure that's who sings it?" I asked again.

"Yes. Why?"

"Well, you're not going to believe this, but..." I told her the whole story. After we hung up I ran to the computer to print up the lyrics. The message was vibrantly clear.

~No one can get in the way of what I'm feeling. No one can get in the way of what I feel for you.~

Alicia Keys—I'll be darned. I supposed *keys to the car* wasn't the only reference to the word *keys.* Amazing. Could my day get any better? "I love you" was how I felt my morning started.

Later in the day, I shared the experience again. This time with Megan. "I'm in wow-wow land right now," I started. "The song fits me and him to a tee. It's beautiful in one sense, but so terribly sad in this physical aspect of me being here, and him being over there. There are no words that can expertly describe my sorrow. But can you believe it? Keys?"

"The two of you make me laugh," she chuckled. "That's so cool, Keys."

I thought it was neat, too. Even though it was a great highlight for the day, I had a new concern. The vibration thing going on in my feet—I couldn't figure it out.

"I need to ask you a question, Megan. Is it possible, even remotely possible, that Chip has left a part of his energy inside of me? I may be way off and sound a little wacky, but let me try to explain."

"I'll never forget the experience when that watermelon shaped ball of energy entered my chest. I was reminded of it again this morning when it was switched on by that song. I have these odd vibrations in my feet and even my legs at times."

"Sometimes I say things I wouldn't normally say; it'll sound more like Chip. And when I hear it come out, I laugh. I've even caught myself rubbing my chin for no reason and when I realize I'm doing it, I think about how it's something he did. I'm sure we can squash these easily, but here's the doozey."

"I had an astonishing experience the other day. I try so hard not to think of *that* fatal morning, but on this day I was doing just that. I turned down my street coming home and when I did, I had this intense feeling of fear. I've never felt something so horrid in all of my life. My heart raced faster than it ever has. It was so intense, I literally lost my breath."

"As quickly as it began though, it stopped. It lasted for about three or four full seconds, the longest seconds ever. My immediate reaction—I sensed the killer's adrenaline. I even said it out loud, 'I don't want to know how he felt. I want *nothing* to do with him.'"

"And then I told Chip's mom about it and she thought I felt Chip, not the evil man. Being that it lasted for a couple of seconds—that makes sense. Is it possible I felt what he experienced right before he was shot? Is it possible he has a part of his energy inside of me? Is this why I feel no anger for his passing? I should be feeling anger by now, don't you think? But he's kept me so busy I haven't felt hatred or anger. Is all of this because of him?"

I wondered briefly if she might think I was a complete lunatic now. I was hoping she'd understand. She'd seen more than I'd ever see or hear... surely, she would.

"About the energy. Everything we touch leaves our energy," she explained. "For example, last night my dad lost the stone from his ring. I told him to focus his energy on the stone rather than the ring, and when he did, he found it right away. I think it's possible that's what's happening to you. Not that he left something behind, but that you will always have a piece of him with or in you."

"About the fear. Everything that has ever been thought still exists. That's how a few mediums say they've connected. But they're connecting to the thought form rather than the energy of the person. This is when you know it's off because of the fear that can come through with them; they're not connected to the other side, but to this side. Much like the other medium saying your life was in danger. I think in your *not* trying to think about that morning, you did, and you picked up Chip."

"Only it wasn't him, it was those thoughts he was having."

Okay, his energy was still inside of me. That made sense. So I connected with his thoughts of that horrible morning. Not him per se, just his thoughts. Huh, how'd I do that?

"So what you're saying is... I do have his energy inside of me and I always will. Am I feeling him or am I feeling his energy that's been left with me? I know—I'm weird, but let me give you another example."

"There are times when I think about him never walking

through the front door and then this unbelievable sadness sweeps over me. I think about how I'll never see him again and then the torment climbs in. I'll start crying with the most intense degree of despair."

"Suddenly, I can feel him standing in the room. Or I can feel him passing by. Or walking through the room. I can't see him, but I know he's there. I *know* he's there. With that, my attention is instantly grabbed and I feel nothing but his love. And then that massive feeling of love removes the hopeless sadness and instead of crying, I move through the house, allowing my curiosity to stroll on a search for him."

"I never find him, but I do feel him. And just like that, he's taken my misery away for that brief moment. I don't feel the sorrow until later, when I start thinking again about how he died. And then the same process is repeated again. He literally stops me from being blue. So am I feeling his energy that's been left with me—or am I feeling him?"

"I feel like what you're feeling *is* him. And it's not that you're not supposed to feel something, but the limited way we think of death is not the limited way *they* experience it," Megan said.

The limited way we think of death isn't the limited way they experience it—was this why he had me feeling him instead of the pain? Was he not experiencing the same kind of torment that was ripping me apart? He couldn't be. Because whenever he was near, he made my sadness flee into curiosity.

"Okay, thank you. Do you mind if I run something else by you? Another dream?" I asked.

"Of course not."

"I didn't give it as much credit as it deserved at first. But the more I thought about it, the more alive it became. In a past life, I think I died before Chip."

"I saw him sitting at a huge round table. He was with three other men, his friends, and they were playing cards. This was odd because Chip wouldn't play cards. It was a holiday tradition in my family, but he wanted no part of it. Anyway, he was rough looking, unshaved, and he had reddish blond hair."

"I had come into the room where he sat, when I was ambushed with the adoration and the same love we have today. I had gotten out of bed when I wasn't supposed to—I was deathly ill."

"Everything around me reminded me of a period long, long ago. I saw the walls made of wood. I'm certain it was a log cabin. I wore a long white, slip-like gown made of cotton; old-style clothing. The table the men sat at was solid wood. It was thick and old with a huge barrel underneath. And the dimly lit room was filled with cigar smoke."

"I walked over to him and he looked at me with great concern. He said, 'Sweetie, you don't look like you feel well. You need to go back and lie down.'"

"And I replied, 'I know. But I wanted to see you. I'll go back to bed now.' I was pale white. I could see me through his eyes. I kissed him on the lips and then I watched me as I left to return to bed. I was very sick. I could feel it inside. And that's it. That's all I remember. I think I died from that illness. Sometimes Megan, I don't think I make a lick of sense."

"You have no idea how much sense you do make," she said. "It sounds like the dream was a past life, it feels that way. Like I said, the two of you have been together many, many times. The way you two communicate will continue to change."

"I have no idea how much sense I do make?" Seriously? Inside this head of mine, I often wondered if I hadn't cracked up completely. I spent entirely too much time trying to put myself inside of Chip's shoes, but I couldn't fathom his

experience. How could I? I was alive and he—he was dead.

"Is it normal to experience sexual feelings or desires in dream-visits or talk about sex? The reason I ask is because when I woke up this morning, I questioned what Chip was trying to share."

"He was lying next to me in bed and I had the TV on. A dirty movie was playing when I noticed the volume was too loud. When I turned it down, he opened his eyes and then asked, 'Is that why we didn't have sex for two weeks during Christmas?'"

"I answered him, 'Yes, but I thought you didn't want to and also, we didn't want to have sex in case it hurt me.'"

"It felt like a big communication error between us, Megan, but it also felt like I had gone through a difficult surgery and we weren't supposed to have sex. It was really weird, and not remotely true."

"The next thing I saw, out of nowhere, we were standing inside the kitchen. But we had company. A young boy with a small learning disability was there as well. Chip and the little guy drew a masterpiece on an *Etch A Sketch* and I was helping the boy hang it on the refrigerator. When I glanced at it, I noticed he had written, *Lyn is a horse.*"

"I looked at Chip and acted like I was insulted even though I wasn't. I said, 'He wrote I'm a horse.' Chip's smile vanished when an upset look took its place, playfully of course, and then he walked over to observe. When he inspected the board, the words were gone. The little boy had erased the comment and *giraffe* was written in its place."

"I saw it too and giggled. I continued to help the boy hang his *Etch A Sketch* while I watched Chip walk back to the counter. He folded his arms across his chest and smiled from ear to ear. He was proud of something but I couldn't tell if it was me or the boy."

"While he watched my every move, I sensed the power of his love. He was wrapped in it while extending it outside of his aura in order to physically touch me. My breath was literally swept away. And the little boy—he belonged to us somehow. He was our responsibility to take care of."

"And then bam, I was awake. I was never so happy to see Chip but at the same time, I couldn't help but wonder about the little guy. Is that not the weirdest dream?"

Chapter Twenty-Five

Déjà VU

"Your grief cycle may be similar to the stages *Elizabeth Kubler-Ross* wrote about, but it is yours alone. Don't worry about what you feel and don't feel, just feel it. You may never be angry, or it may come in years. It's your life and your grief, and it may be different from anyone else's," said Megan.

"We have all been taught that death is final, and if our loved ones are there, they can't be here and vice versa. We've been taught that our relationship is over when someone passes, and that death is black and white."

"We have time and space limitations here, our loved ones do not. They can be in several places, doing several things at the same time. There is no time or concept of time and no matter how long you've been apart, it will seem like only fifteen minutes when you reunite. We can have an even better relationship with them on the other side than we had while they were here. Our thoughts of them will bring them to us."

"As a part of your grief, missing him sexually is normal; so it's normal, yes. It sounds as if the dreams are a pre-cursor to the waking, like his visits to you were the pre-cursor to your waking visits," Megan said.

Okay. I need to re-train my entire thought process. If I could do that, change my thoughts, there was a real possibility to have a continued relationship. Yes, that's what I wanted. No, correction. It's what I desired. I had no idea who Elizabeth Kubler-Ross was, either. It didn't take long to look her books up online and order, "Is There Life After Death?"

I knew I couldn't change the past; it was done. Chip was gone and I was here. If I wanted to talk to him, I knew I needed to change my reaction to what was happening around me.

Hunger. I had an undeniable hunger to do whatever I had to do. Whether it'd be in mediumship, meditation, joining a spiritual church—it didn't matter. I desired to be as close to him as I could get. And no one was going to stop me. This stubborn goat insisted on communicating with her dead lover. One way or another...

There were lots of days of sadness. It was only months since his death, so naturally the overwhelming distress imprisoned me. There were many days it didn't seem to matter what he did. I ignored him completely and dove into depression. I curled up in bed more times than I can count and cried relentlessly. There wasn't any denying it... my heartache was my new normal.

I did something off the wall one day; I knew better, but I couldn't stop myself. I picked up the phone and dialed Megan. I was ashamed I hadn't asked her for an appointment or warn her. I prayed she answered. Something had flown into my thoughts and I needed to ask her a quick question.

"Déjà vu—I've had them all my life," I said. "My sister as well. I had so many with Chip that it literally sparked a conversation between us about the afterlife and religion. Whenever I experienced them, I always thought I was doing what I was supposed to be doing at that moment."

"Since reading all these books about souls, and if I'm to believe we choose our lives before birth, it makes me think that déjà vu is a screening process. Maybe it's a trigger mode when I feel them. Is this right?"

"Totally!" she exclaimed. "I have them all the time. I've heard lots of explanations, but to me they're a signal that I'm on the right track."

"Well, I had one last night in bed reading. It felt like I had already lived that moment before, yet it was the first time ever experiencing it. This would mean Chip was meant to die when he did. It was his time to go even if I refuse to believe it was. Right?"

"I feel like you're right about Chip, yes," she agreed. "Had he not gone on that day, something else would have happened. His agreement for this side was complete though he wasn't consciously expecting it. That's the confusion bit. But he adjusted quickly and went to work on fulfilling the agreement the two of you made about communicating across time, space, and death. Way cool if you ask me."

I wasn't as excited as Megan about the speed of his abilities. I still wished, badly, that he was here in person and not as a spirit. Yet, I had to admit it was amazing how quickly he adjusted and went to work communicating and waking me up.

What agreement was she talking about? Did I dare ask what she meant? Was I ready for something new, something more I had to try and wrap my head around?

No, not yet. Not today.

It was comforting enough to know I was normal experiencing the déjà vu's. I often wondered if they were a window of something I observed before I was born. Or if they were reflections my higher-self, my soul, was allowing me to visually see.

If they were a window or a reflection, did that mean I was traveling the right path? Was I doing exactly what I was supposed to be doing at that exact moment? Was I unable to change the outcome because the experience was already preordained, set in stone?

Or did it mean the déjà vu was a path I had already traveled? Maybe in a different life? Or a multiple life? Or quite possibly an opportunity to change the direction I was headed?

It was hard enough to accept Chip's death the way he died. But to know via a déjà vu his murder was meant to happen exactly the way it happened?

Honestly, how was I supposed to accept that?

Chapter Twenty-Six

MY SISTER

That same evening, my sister and I played phone tag. I tried her one last time before going to bed, when she answered. I had no idea the surprise that awaited me.

"What's wrong? You sound too quiet," I asked.

"Something happened last night. Something I've never experienced before and I'm still trying to process it. You know how you're getting more comfortable experiencing your dreams with Chip?"

"Yes..."

"I think he visited me last night," she told me.

"Are you serious? Did he talk to you?"

"Not really. It was a lot like a movie. I was riding in a very loud car, sitting in the back seat, but I swear I was floating. We turned into a driveway that led onto a bumpy dirt road. That bumpy road—it stood out like a sore thumb. The car was shaking me around so hard that all I wanted was for it to stop."

"We then drove into a field that was pitch black. At first I couldn't see anything, it was so dark out. When I looked over to the side though, I saw Chip. I could see his truck. And then that's when I saw you standing there."

"Lyn, you looked so beautiful. So at peace. The two of you were standing there side-by-side. You weren't doing anything, just looking at me. Then, all of a sudden, whoever I was with, took off."

"Oh my God, that car was so loud, Lyn. And then came the

bumps again, for the second time. That road was so bumpy; I could feel every single one of them."

"We made a right-hand turn out onto the road and that's when the car got even louder. The driver floored it. All I could hear was a loud noise filling up the car; I had to cover my ears. I was staring out the windshield as we made an immediate U-turn and the driver hit the accelerator again. We were hauling ass, traveling down a long, long road."

"There were two people inside the car. I watched them change their clothes in the front seat. And then I asked, 'What's going on here? Why am I sitting here in this car?' Instantly, I left."

"The next thing I know I'm standing in front of a casket. The one Chip was in at the funeral home. I said to him, 'Oh no, Chip. You can't come jumping out of that box because you will scare the heck out of me.'"

"And just like that, everything went dark. I couldn't see anything. But then, through that darkness, only feet in front of me, I see Chip. I only see his face. He was smiling and looking so at peace. Everything went black again—and poof, he was gone."

There was a moment of silence before I realized she had nothing more to add. "Wow, that was different, sister. Did it scare you?" I asked.

"No, not really. I was so focused on trying to see inside that lot. When I did see the two of you standing next to each other, I knew everything was going to be okay. I didn't get scared again until I was standing in front of Chip's casket. That's when I knew he was going to scare the living day lights out of me if he opened up his eyes."

Her experience was called, *a third-party message*. I had read that somewhere recently. It's considered third-party when a loved one visits someone other than you. That loved one may deliver a message directly for you, or they may show something that will ultimately find its way to you.

Was there a message inside my sister's visit?

I couldn't find one. I didn't understand why she was taken to that big empty lot. Or why she had to ride in that loud car. To top it off, her description of how she traveled didn't match that of the detectives. They said the murderer traveled west and never made a U-turn.

The next time my sister visited, I took her for a ride but didn't share where we were headed. As soon as I pulled into the driveway of the lot where Chip was gunned down, she screamed.

"Oh my God, Lyn. This is it, isn't it?"

I didn't say a word, not yet. After we traveled over several of the bumps she had described, she became ill quite suddenly.

"I was here!" she yelled. "This is where you and Chip were standing. Right here!"

Chapter Twenty-Seven

HAPPY ANNIVERSARY

T he next morning, my eyes opened slowly to the new day while expressing their complete displeasure. As I took that first blink, I heard a voice… singing.

"Happy Anniversary, baby. Got you on my mind."

Only eight words. Nothing else. I was groggy, but I smiled because Chip had wished me a Happy Anniversary. I tried to remember today's date. It was the fifth of April.

"Okay, it must be our anniversary. But didn't you recently say that every day was our anniversary?" I questioned him, out loud.

Something special must have happened last year and I tried to remember what it was. But I couldn't think of anything. I went to the year before that one. Nothing. And the year before that one. Again, nothing.

I became frustrated. To the hilt. I rolled out of bed and rushed to the kitchen for coffee. Every day was our anniversary, he said so weeks ago. There had to be a reason for this particular date though, yet I had no clue what the motive was.

The message was beautiful—he had me on his mind—but the morning was a horrible one and I went back to bed. Nothing I did stopped the tears from tumbling. Missing Chip was at the tip of the day.

"I can't stand living here without you," I yelled out.

I tried to be strong. I wanted to be a part of his continued life. I wanted to receive his communications and be grateful for all of them. But this morning, I buried my face into the pillow to cry. And then out of nowhere, I heard his voice whisper.

"Writing—you must write. We're going to make a big difference in millions of people's lives. We're going to help many realize that life isn't the end of who we are."

I rolled over and instantly shouted, "Where the hell did that come from?" I glanced over at his side of the bed, but he wasn't there. I lay still, contemplating now, wide awake.

Did I dare believe the voice I'd heard? He wants me to write? We're going to help how many people? Millions? "That's insane!" I yelled, disbelieving all of it. But Chip didn't say another word.

For the second time, I got out of bed, let the kids out, and got a drink of water. I stood in the kitchen staring blankly at the sofa where Chip normally sat. His words were screaming loud inside my head—*you must write*.

But that was the last thing I wanted to do. I tapped my foot defiantly. Yet, letting him down wasn't going to happen either. "If that's what you want me to do, I should begin, yes?"

"Yes..." I heard in a soft whisper.

"Okay. There you have it, Lyn," I said, out loud.

I pulled a TV table up close, placed the laptop on it, opened a new document, and then sat with my fingers on the keyboard. Suddenly, I realized all of my notes were sitting inside the car.

After grabbing the key, I unlocked the car, walked outside, reached for the car door—but it was surprisingly, locked.

"Well that's odd," I voiced.

So I went back inside, picked up the remote again and repeated the whole process the same way. This time I *heard* the door lock as I approached the car, but I reached for it anyway—yes, the car had locked itself, again.

"Okay. This isn't funny," I said firmly.

"Is this really happening?"

I decided to try it again. And then again. Each time arriving at the same result. Finally, I sat on the front steps and laughed.

"Are you having fun, Chip?" I asked, out loud.

Goose bumps covered my arms. It was Chip, playing. I darted back inside, grabbed the remote, took it with me to the car and this time, it unlocked. I quickly gathered my notes and went back inside. I was on top of the world and filled with joy. It almost suffocated me. To be that close to Chip and his goofy self—I was soaring with delicious delight.

After calming down and returning to the laptop, I put my thinking cap on. What was I supposed to say? I had no experience writing or telling a story and God knows, I had no idea how to write a book. When I was a kid I dreamed of writing a fiction novel some day, but personally, I thought this was a crazy idea and not a smart thing to do. But Chip wanted me to write and I had already promised that I would.

The only thing I could come up with was to begin by sharing his death. The first sentence appeared; *I would have never thought it.* And then the second; *Not in a million years.* I wrote the third one; *To wake up to the sound of love, only to experience unspeakable tragedy minutes later...*

I exploded into tears, unable to write another word. Instead, I slammed myself into the couch and cried for an hour. It was just too hard. I had put so much effort toward not thinking about *that* day and now? He wanted me to describe it? Seriously, what was he thinking?

Once the tears subsided, I got up, grabbed the key remote, and headed outside to play. That made me feel better. That made me closer to Chip. I wanted to be with him. No matter where he was...

And now I had a direct link—the car. When I felt the need to talk to him, to see him, or to hear from him, I ran outside with the remote. Each time, I was taken to an instant height of euphoria. I had my very own secret link to Chip.

The gloom and doom was gone.

I thought about sharing my newfound link with Megan, but hesitated. If she told me it wasn't Chip, my joy would forever be crushed. A couple of days later though, I gave in.

"Man, did I ever crash this past weekend," I told her. "I truly took ten steps backward. I was so bad that I was on my hands and knees begging Chip for a sign Saturday morning."

I described the game with the car and then asked, "Can this be him? Not some earthbound playing head games with me? I asked Chip if it was him. As soon as I did, I was instantly covered in chills."

"You know it's him," she said. "Earthbounds don't have enough energy to do that over and over. Besides, when you asked if it was Chip, you got an immediate reply. I'm sorry you had a rough couple of days, that's bound to happen. Although this car door thing has kept you distracted, what a gift."

"A gift?" she had stunned me. "I never thought of it that way. Shame on me. The experience was so exciting that I failed to look at it in any other way but complete elation."

"Hey, Megan, after I jot down a few notes about something that happened before Chip died, and then compare it to what's happened these past few days—may I call you?"

"Dreams these are not. I'm having horrible nightmares."

Chapter Twenty-Eight

TUG OF WAR

My short novel began. I wrote it all down and emailed it instead of calling her. Keeping a calm voice would probably not occur. I was digging deep inside and being completely honest with my feelings.

I wrote, "In December, I had three bad dreams. They were the first vivid dreams I'd ever had and I shared them with Chip. After the third one though, he expressed grave concern. He said, 'Maybe we need to get you some help.' He told me it wasn't normal for someone to have dreams about death. I considered them nightmares. He was worried, but I laughed it off and told him I didn't need help."

"The next month he was murdered by a co-worker. We haven't even mentioned the word *intuition*. The Tuesday before he died, I heard my inner voice. She was so loud and so crystal clear when she said, 'You need to call Damone and give him this load.'"

"But what did I say back? I said, *I'll wait until tomorrow— he can haul it then.* I was sick with a bad cold and all I had on my mind was getting home to Chip. I wanted to be with him and nothing else mattered. If I would have listened to that voice, Chip wouldn't have been shot the next morning because the man who did it would have been in Fort Pierce at 5:00 a.m.—four hours away."

"I live with this every single day. I could have given Chip a different exit plan. I read somewhere that we have at least three exits to choose from. If this is true, Chip would have used a different one instead of *that* one on *that* day."

"Nevertheless, I know I can't change what happened. I can think about his death, like I do, from the minute I wake up until the minute I fall asleep. But the one thing I must do in the future is make sure I don't miss another signal or another sign. I never, ever, want to make that mistake again—hence the reason behind this quandary."

"Last Thursday, I had a horrible nightmare. I won't go into detail because I actually grossed my sister out when I shared it with her. But it did end in death. I was in the dream and I was killed as well. Not me as Lyn, but as someone else."

"Saturday night I had another nightmare. That one involved military soldiers and I was one of them, only I was a man. Every soldier was killed in the dream, including me. We were ambushed by the Russians. Our position had been leaked by someone on our side, the United States."

"When I woke from that dream, I became scared. Not because of the nightmare, but because of what happened in December. Since this is April, I immediately linked it to the possibility of someone dying in May. If I was having death dreams again, I figured they had to be a sign."

"I know it sounds weird. And I know you don't read bad things, but I truly don't understand why I have nightmares like these. I'm a good person, I really am. I don't have wicked thoughts or mean intentions. Heck, I don't even hate the person who murdered the love of my life. I know Chip is behind that—he's keeping me focused on other things instead of his murder."

"Intuition should have saved Chip. I failed him badly. My heart rips into pieces with every breath I take. He loves me dearly, I know this. He's trying to heal me because he knows I could have done something to save him—and I didn't. Chip knows I want it to be me who died... not him. Not like that."

"I guess what I'm asking is this—what do these dreams of death mean? Am I seeing how people are being killed? Am I supposed to warn someone else to be careful? There was no one in either dream that I knew. The first one however, the killer's name was Dan. He was a manager at a Winn Dixie and had been working there for two years."

"With the help of his elderly female friend, he organized the kidnapping of several young people, taking them into the middle of nowhere and then violently killing them. I was one of his victims. Before he brutally murdered me, I managed to cut my finger and wrote a message in blood on the backseat of his car. *I'm Karen. Dan murdered me.* I remember everything about that man, Dan, but I don't know him in real life."

"Or do you think it's time I seek help?"

I clicked the send button and headed to the kitchen for a drink. Those dreams had warped my mind. As hard as I tried to forget them, I couldn't. Like the dreams back in December, I needed to know if they were a warning of something coming in the near future.

My feelings were if I'd paid attention in December, maybe I could have saved Chip from being shot. Maybe I could have sensed something bad was about to happen and possibly redirected our lives. But since I didn't see that then, it was my desire to make sure I didn't miss anything today.

Before bed, I checked for a reply.

Megan had responded, "I'm going to sleep on this and meditate on it. I will respond tomorrow. I don't think you need help, and I don't think you need to be Johnny from *The Dead Zone* warning people."

"I get hits like that at times and have learned that to ask for those to be turned off but not to anything else, it doesn't work."

My answer would come tomorrow.

I waited all day to hear, but nothing came. Megan was a busy lady; I knew that, so I laid low. After finishing a long day at work, I drove home in silence. My release of sadness in the car was still ongoing. However, the time allotted had been reduced to an hour instead of two most days. Today of all days, would bring a rather interesting surprise though. I would experience a heartbeat that would shoot from a flat zero to a sudden fifty in a rapid flash.

When I walked up to the screen door on my front patio—it was open. It wasn't just unlocked; it was open by about a foot. To know me, would be to know my avid routine is to lock the doors without fail, never, ever, skipping this ritual. You could say I was a little anal that way.

Yet, today the door wasn't only unlocked, it was freely accessible to swing open if a breeze were to catch it. And to boot? The only key to this door was mine.

After checking the main door—*locked*—I rushed inside to check on the kids. They were fine and happy to see me. There was no explanation about the door being opened, so I figured either one, I didn't lock it—*unlikely*—or two, it was Chip leaving a surprise, not sure.

As we headed outside my phone rang; it was Megan.

"Okay, here we go," she said. "I think you're gifted, really psychic. I think you're opening up with Chip's help, and you're picking up extraneous stuff."

"Last summer, two days before the bridge collapsed in Minnesota, I had a dream that a bridge collapsed. I didn't know where or when, just that it would happen. Three days before the mine collapsed and all of those miners were killed, I dreamt of a black tunnel, and men coughing and dying. Again, I didn't know where or when, just that it would happen."

"On 9/11, I had a dream, and when the Tsunami struck in December 2004, I had a dream. It messed me up because I thought I should have been able to do something. Occasionally, as I pass by someone on the street, I can see things they wouldn't want me to see, like terrible abuse. This was getting to me and I was afraid every day of what I would see. I struck up a deal with my guides that unless I can, and am supposed to do something about it, they would tell me rather than me see it."

"Recently, I did a ghost busting in Michigan. There was a terrible sick entity in the house that during his life did awful things to children and to animals. My guides; bless them, told me about the abuses rather than me having to watch a movie in my mind about them."

"We can't ask to not see this stuff, but we can find another way to deal with it. This is what I think is happening to you. Chip's death, and everything leading up to it, activated something so that you are picking up on more. I know it's a difficult feeling and a helpless feeling, but unless you're supposed to do something about it, which in this case you would be seeing more, you can turn it over to the angels, or your guides, or to Chip, because it is out of your hands."

"I think it will be a while before this world is free of violence. So many people are focused on it and continue to activate it. In the meantime, all we can do is ask for assistance from a Being or spirit who can do something for us, and then let it go. At first it seems hard, but then you develop an even better relationship with your angels and guides. They would love to assist and work with you—they just need to be asked. Have you read any of Doreen Virtue's books yet?"

"No, I'm sorry, not yet. But I did order a couple," I said.

"That's good. I think they'll help you. Another thing, you and Chip had this agreement in this lifetime for what happened to happen. Yes, you did get signals and messages that at that time you put aside. These may have resulted in a different outcome, but he still would have left, just by another way."

"The opportunity, and I imagine it doesn't seem like one right now, is to be connected to the Source, God, Universe; whatever you want to call it. To listen and heed the messages in the future."

"I keep saying, Lyn, you are going to make a powerful difference for people out of this. Chip wants you to write. He says if all you can do is take ten or fifteen minutes every day to write, that will be good enough. He's with you, helping."

I was speechless. Where did this angel come from? She was always telling me exactly what I needed to hear. And it made perfect sense. Again, I was reminded once more to write.

"Megan, I know you're right, I heard it again today—keep writing my love, keep writing—I know he wants me to write, but gosh, it's so hard. I'll try and put those dreams to rest. But wow, what powerful stuff they were. And incredibly sick people. Thank you so much for helping me. I don't know what I'd do without you. Do you have another minute? Can I run another dream by you?"

"Yes, of course."

"Well, I don't think this was a dream. I think it was something else. I was trying to meditate the other day like you taught me. I closed my eyes, relaxed deeply, when a bunch of faces started popping up in front of me. But this one boy— there was one boy who did something extraordinary."

"The night before, I had watched a show about spring-breakers whose vacations ended in death. The program was about the parents searching for justice for their kids. One boy, who was either eighteen or nineteen, lived in Ontario, Canada. He went on spring break to Cancun, Mexico."

"He was found murdered on the beach in the early morning hours and out of nowhere, there he was. Standing in front of me. Talking to me. He said, 'Tell the police to talk to ____. She did not do this to me, but she knows who did.'"

"And then right before he disappeared, he said, 'Oh, and she's a prostitute.' I felt my body jerk when he said that, but I made sure to tell him, 'Okay. I'll make sure I remember her name.' But guess what? I forgot her name. I did remember it beginning with an SH sound though."

"So yesterday, I was making my appointments at work. I was on the phone with a lady and asked her to repeat her name. She said, 'Sharlee.' That's not a common name. I laid the phone down and sat in shock and then screamed, 'That's the name that boy told me!'"

"I'm too scared to write a letter to the Ontario Police Department saying, 'Hey, by the way, I had a dream about this guy named Mark who was murdered. You need to find so-and-so because she knows what happened to him.' They'll think I'm nuts. Should I do anything about this or should I file it away?"

Megan responded, "I would look for confirmation for yourself first. Unfortunately, the medium and psychic things that come through are still weird for people and we wouldn't want them to look to you as a suspect. Try to find newspaper stories about the murder. If you do find something, you may want to pursue, but I wouldn't go the police route. It doesn't feel right. And if you can find information about this man, then you know you've got real info."

"I think you're right," I told her. "You know what else? Today is the first day since Chip died that I haven't bawled for hours. I'm not saying tears haven't crossed my eyes and I'll admit, I sat in the car and cried for about ten minutes. But I normally sit there for an hour or more bawling, talking to Chip before I go in the house."

"Today… I actually feel blessed. To have this man stay here by my side, trying to make me feel better, I'm so perfectly blessed. I even told him, 'how can I continue to be so sad when it's still you and me? Whatever's going to happen in the future will still be you and me—but in a different way.'"

"You got it," she agreed. "When we can turn our focus from missing their physicalness to developing a new relationship, that's when the real gift starts. At some point, you'll know and feel that what you have now is even better than what you had while both of you were here."

For days I searched looking for more information about the young boy. My attempts failed miserably. There was nothing anywhere. It was so sad …

He was so visible and quite clear in what he said.

186

Chapter Twenty-Nine

TALK TO ME

C hip was still being funny. Trying to make me laugh. One
morning, I woke up when I heard a few words drag out
in slow motion. The words skipped across the room right into
my thoughts.

"I'm so bald over here."

I couldn't help it. I laughed. Poor guy. He was so worried
about going bald. He even had me worried about it as well.

That same evening, I heard his voice again.

Lying in bed, propped up against his pillow, staring at his
picture pasted to my laptop, I was deep in thought. The tears
were rushing forward, but I didn't want to cry. For just one
evening, I wanted to *not* soak my pillow. Instead, I wanted to
be happy he was still with me.

"Talk to me, damn it…" a voice shouted.

That voice was so loud it frightened me. I threw the laptop
across the bed and immediately jumped up, unmoving. But
then, I had to laugh. It was Chip. Talking to me.

He was there watching me, listening to my thoughts, yet I
couldn't see him anywhere. I instantly chatted back. There was
no question he could hear me. There was no doubt he was
beside me yearning for me to understand.

Our love hadn't died, only his body. But this was hard. It
was difficult to talk to someone I loved deeply and not have
him physically in front of me speaking back. For an hour, I

unloaded my feelings to my invisible lover, and then laid my head down to sleep.

That next morning I awakened anxious to pick up Scooby.

The day before, I had dropped him off to be neutered. This was something Chip and I had wanted to do together, but that wasn't possible now. Alone, I had to fight forward. In addition, Scooby needed to calm down—I was hoping this would help.

He had turned into a real wild child. I didn't realize just how much so until three hours before his scheduled pick up time. The vet had called and literally begged me to come in early and retrieve him. His behavior was a disruption to all of the other dogs—that wasn't a very good sign.

I also had an appointment later in the day. I was gearing up for a psychic reading with Megan. A psychic reading was different than a medium reading. It would be more about me and my life's purpose and not so much about Chip. This was something new and I was excited to learn more.

After getting Scooby settled in, I took a ride to ensure privacy and parked in an open lot under a big shady oak tree. A few minutes later, I dialed Megan's number. As the phone rang, I glanced up. Something mysterious was sitting in front of me.

There were three tiny fish drawings—painted on the *inside* of the windshield.

"Well how can that be?" I leaned in closer. "How odd."

I stared at them in wonder until Megan answered and then focused on the call. Sitting back in the seat, I relaxed and enjoyed my first ever psychic reading experiencing lots of chill bumps—my new sign of truth.

Almost immediately afterwards, my attention went back to the windshield and the drawings.

"I swear these are fish pictures. But how did they get

there?" I was in utter disbelief. "Chip, did you do that?"

There were two and a half fish… drawn clearly. Each the size of a quarter maybe. I studied them for a long time and then decided to drive home to be with Scooby. After giving him his medicine, he soon went to sleep. Having forgotten about the fish, I decided to go to bed, too. It had been a packed day.

Beside me was a man. He was wise, older, a gentle soul. We were standing on a stage. Soon, it would be my turn to go out and speak in front of a large group of people. Or maybe we were both going, I couldn't be sure.

He grabbed my elbow and gently pulled me toward him. I stared out into the crowd as he began whispering in my ear.

"Just remember this," he said softly, "Everything that comes through the ear, goes to the heart."

"Oh wow," I whispered back, "That's really good. I have to write that down so I don't forget it."

I pulled out my notepad and turned it sideways. His statement was important and I knew I needed to document it. I scribbled the words sideways across the pad with a blue pen.

~Just remember this. Everything that comes through the ear …goes to the heart.~

Chapter Thirty

BABY STEPS

The following weekend, I decided to nap. It was a stressful week at work and catching up on sleep seemed important. Plus, it led me to Chip as well. I always hoped for a visit because it was such a joy to see his handsome face.

I was still groggy when I got out of bed and could hear the TV blaring from the living room. Amazingly, I didn't think it odd at the time. I paraded into the hall bathroom and proceeded to brush my hair up into a ponytail, and then brushed my teeth. At the same time, my thoughts were direct and very clear.

Chip needs to turn that TV down. It's too loud.

After taking a few steps forward into the hallway, I heard a loud click. The TV had mysteriously been shut off and my forward progress had halted. I stopped in my tracks and listened to the dead silence. There wasn't a sound coming from anywhere. And then it hit me.

"Nothing's changed," I said. "He's still here watching TV."

I walked over to the television to see if it was warm. It wasn't. I turned to stare at the sofa to see if he was there; he wasn't.

Nothing had changed … yet everything had changed.

There were two sets of emotions I experienced these days. One, I hauled ass down the highway of grief. When I got into it, I was inside of it bad. Chip couldn't stop the ocean of tears or fix my brittle and broken heart even if he wanted to. It was something I had to go through. And I knew that.

The second emotion was one where I felt exhilarated every time Chip showed me his heart of love. Imagining him gone and not always around, it was unthinkable now. I wanted him close. I wanted him to show me how alive he was, to share things with me, and to help guide me to the ending of this physical life. Until he left or took a back seat, all of my energy was sunk into him. It was the only way I knew to move forward.

And then I set a new goal for myself.

No more sitting in the car crying for hours.

Today, I was going to push myself right out that door. It was time to end the agony that was being inflicted. I had punished myself for far too long. Going cold-turkey wasn't going to happen, but to reduce the time to a couple of days a week instead of everyday—definite progress.

Baby steps, Lyn. Baby steps...

The kids were in high spirits to see me early. We hopped and skipped and jumped around like mad. I was determined to find a little joy somewhere.

After their duties were completed, I headed to the fridge with Scooby at my heels. He waited patiently while I filled the water bowl. Angel was busy cleaning her feet on the kitchen rug beside us.

Tap—Tap—Tap

The sound was loud. And it was coming from their room, a breakfast nook with a bay window. Angel sprung off, yapping all the way. Scooby took a second to think about it, but decided to join her. Together, they barked loudly, their tails wagging frantically.

There wasn't a person in sight. There was nothing there. I did the only thing I knew to do. I laughed, out loud. After their water bowl was filled, I watched Angel jump all around inside their big bed. The bottom had a plastic lining and that was where the tapping originated.

To the naked eye, it looked as though she were searching for whatever or whoever made the noise. I had a sneaking suspicion though, she wasn't looking for anything. It was so obvious. Their daddy was playing with them and in that moment—it was priceless. And extremely magical.

Once everything calmed, my thoughts went back to the fish drawings located on the windshield. I decided to grab my camera and head outside. It was easy to lose track of time as I spent more than an hour studying the little drawings. From the camera display, they looked very cute.

A couple of hours later, I grabbed my phone and called Megan to tell her what I'd discovered.

"Megan, can loved ones draw pictures from the other side?"

"They can definitely draw pictures," she said. "They can do whatever they want. That's really neat."

Chip was certainly keeping me on my toes. Always. But drawings? On the inside of the windshield? It really was neat, but very odd. He certainly had my undivided attention.

When morning came, I experienced another of those message of words dance across my thoughts. It was a song, playing in my head. The words were clear as day.

"Don't stop believing. Hold onto that feeling."

"I haven't heard that song in a long time. What, years?" I whispered, to no one. The song was one of my favorites by Journey. Those few words played over and over, like a broken record. *Don't stop believing. Hold onto that feeling.*

And then my phone rang. It was my sister.

She had taken it upon herself to acquire Chip's place in the mornings. She never missed a beat. When 4:30 a.m. rolled around, she was right there to chat. Today, I couldn't wait to share my exciting news about the drawings, the songs, and finally, the car doors locking. I had kept the car-affair a secret, only sharing it with Megan. So I was little surprised when I told her the car locked only at home. I had no proof of that—I hadn't tested that theory yet.

At the time, my sister was a big wig with a large and growing dealership. She was quite the ace when it came to cars. But I didn't expect her to ask me this, "Are you sure there isn't anything wrong with the car?"

It didn't take long to hop on a wagon of defense. "Why would there be? I've never had any trouble with the car except the air conditioner that one time last year."

"Well," she said, "There could be an electrical problem causing the delay in the door lock. I haven't heard of one, but there could be."

I sensed her delicate stride, but I insisted, "I don't think that's it. I think it's Chip playing. The car has never done anything like this before."

As easily as she slid those few words in, we dismissed the subject altogether. I took a shower and moved into the second bathroom to put myself together for work. A few minutes later I was met with yet another message. A song was blasting loudly. I swore it was coming from the radio in another room.

"You are so beautiful, to me. Can't you see? You're everything I've asked for. You're everything I need. You are so beautiful...to me."

I stepped from the sink and dropped to my knees. I didn't want to cry, but there was no stopping it. The tears crashed in and dropped onto the floor.

"What a beautiful song to send me, Chip," I cried out.

"Thank you for loving me!"

For a long while, I just sat and cried. I was sad, yes, but I also recognized that he had kissed me again with his love.

An hour later, I drove into work. My sister's words were bouncing hard inside. I needed to prove her wrong. The car was put into park and a series of tests began. Afterwards, I walked inside with my tail between my legs. The life had literally been sucked right out of me.

I researched the mechanics of the Acura online, but found nothing remotely similar. My world had crashed. I felt completely deflated and suddenly, extremely sad. All signs were leading back to that God-awful grief. If I didn't locate a different perspective, I'd soon straddle that depressive state and dive back in. I knew I had to call my new best friend.

"My sister planted a seed in my head, Megan. After testing the car this morning, I think I have a sensor problem. I told her the doors locked only at home. But it did it here at work today too. Many times. That's not the real concern for me. The real concern was my belief. I believed so madly that Chip was showing me he was communicating through that car. But now I know it wasn't true."

"It's kind of ironic," I continued. "You know that song by Journey, *Don't Stop Believing?* I heard that lyric this morning when I woke up. Do you think Chip was telling me something?"

"I'm sorry you felt disappointed and somewhat invalidated," Megan said, consoling me. "We want so much for everything to be a communication, and so much is. Like why would this happen to your car now? Maybe his message is something specific that many can explain away. Take it in and have it looked over, you never know. That would be my suggestion."

"I think what's important is what you heard, *hold onto that feeling*. It gives you hope and re-assuring. If that's how you feel, who cares what anybody else says," she said.

"That's so true," I agreed. "It doesn't matter what anybody else says, does it? The only thing that matters is what I believe. We only met four years ago. I feel like our time wasn't long enough. We became best of friends before we even developed a serious relationship. Why this connection between the two of us when we didn't share years and years together?"

"I don't think it matters the time spent together or not," she said. "What matters is the connection."

Chip and I had so little time together.

He was snatched away so fast. I knew she was right about it not mattering the time spent together, but I wondered if there was something more. Why was he so adamant I pay attention to him? Would I have sought revenge? Would I have killed the man who killed him?

Or was it because I would have taken my own life? Is that why he was here? To stop me? To wake me up?

"Was I that bad, sweetie?" I asked, out loud.

I was hoping for a signal this time. I was hoping for a sign, a voice, a message... anything. But I heard nothing. I was on my own again.

Flipping through the pages of my crowded mind.

Chapter Thirty-One

HE'S MY BROTHER

For a change of pace, I asked Chip's mom out to dinner. It felt good to see her and spend time together. I knew we were both filled with grief, but it didn't hurt to get out.

Chip was always the subject of our conversation. Little by little it was getting easier to hear stories about his childhood, his Navy career, and the special mother and son memories, too. It killed me to see the tears well up behind her eyes. Not to mention that I was dealing with my own pain, as well. Today however, it was a little easier to talk out loud about him.

We enjoyed a great dinner. Chip and I loved going to *Longhorn Steakhouse*, so it seemed only fitting to take his mom there. At one point, our table light flickered a couple of times, letting us know Chip was there. That was funny. Her eyes went big, her mouth shaped into a complete O, and then she whispered, "Did you see that?" It was an awesome moment.

The dark of night rode in quickly under a starlit sky while I examined the expectation to write again. I couldn't figure out why I was expected to do something I loathed, but I wanted Chip to be proud of me. So I reflected on recent dream-visits and questioned how to present them. One in particular bounced to the front instantly—the little boy who drew on the Etch A Sketch.

Looking up into the dark sky, I became amazed at the number of floating diamonds. There were so many and for a moment I was lost in their beauty. From out of nowhere, I suddenly blurted, "Who is the little boy, Chip? Why was he there? Why him?" Amazingly, seconds later I heard a voice.

"He's my brother..."

It was a distinctive voice with no melody whatsoever. I stood in silence soaking up the message, in awe. And then I heard the male voice again.

"He's my brother..."

This time it was in the form of the song, *He's My Brother,* by Neil Diamond. Just those three little words. "Okay, Chip, I got it. He's your brother, " I whispered.

I gazed at the floating diamonds a bit longer and then felt the need to add, "I feel honored that you brought your brother to meet me. Thank you, my love."

It was straightforward and easy to recognize the importance of the little boy. He was very special. He was Chip's brother.

I walked inside and grabbed the phone.

"Megan, can loved ones still talk to you in a strong tone?"

"Oh sure, why do you ask?"

"Well, last night in bed, I was almost asleep and I remembered I had forgotten to set the alarm on the car. I went back and forth about getting up, but I didn't want to move. I was too comfortable. Out of nowhere, I saw myself standing outside the front door watching three kids break into my car. I warned them off, but then they started shooting at me. I shot back and my bullets landed, but I was also shot. And then poof—the vision was gone."

"I lay still for a minute, stunned, when it slipped out. 'Wow. That was pretty vivid.' I didn't expect to hear anything back, but I did. I heard Chip say, 'Is that what you want to see happen?' I instantly replied, 'No.' And then clear as day, I heard him with a strong force. He said, 'Then get up and go lock the damn door!'"

"His tone was so stern it scared me. I figured I'd better listen, so I got up, turned on the lights, and went and set the alarm. I thought our loved ones mellowed out when they passed. Can Chip still be so loud?"

"Oh sure," she responded. "I feel like it's less common but if necessary, they will. I think comments like that are usually without emotion. Maybe louder so we hear. Sometimes we're comfortable and we aren't listening to the gentle nudges. So we get a louder one."

Okay, so Chip gave me one heck of a push. He freaked me out. He must have been lying right beside me, advising me firmly. That was so strange...

"Does pink represent anything?" I asked Megan. "In a dream last night, we went on a buying mission for another semi-truck that was the brightest shade of pink. Chip would never buy a pink truck, ever. He was too macho for that. But after negotiations about money and freight, we found out the lady had a fleet of trucks for sale and Chip wanted to buy them all—they were all pink. I remember us calling her, the Pink Lady. Pink, pink, pink."

"Love, love, love," she indicated. "They show me pink flowers to communicate love. Pink is the heart Chakra. I think you've been kissed from the other side."

My heart lit up like a bright candle. Chip had kissed me with his love—again. I was the luckiest lady in the world.

My dead fiancé ... was communicating.

Chapter Thirty-Two

VALIDATIONS

There was a gathering for families of victims of murder coming up. Char asked me to accompany her and I couldn't say no. It was a support group with a lot of special people involved. Unfortunately, I felt disjointed there. The focus was more on the murder versus a loved one's continued life and possible afterlife communications. I felt a little out of place and unable to share the mysteries of death.

We also attended a psychic fair that day. That was interesting and where I felt I belonged the most—with individuals who believed and shared the same kind of views. They were very welcoming. There was no preaching or nudging in one direction or another. I engaged in two different styles of readings.

The first reading was a type of stone reading where I had to pick four of them. The first stone symbolized healing, the second was emotions, the third was spirituality, and the fourth was for health.

The reader sat for a bit studying the stones I'd chosen when she acknowledged the emotions. She said, "Your emotions are all over the place. So flip-floppy. You're not able to get a handle on them sometimes."

She had no idea how right she was. She then acknowledged the fourth stone and said, "You're not able to speak out about something yet. You need to find a way to talk about whatever it is, because it's affecting your health. Your spirituality has been lifted, yet your health is more important." Again, she had no clue how spot on she was.

At one point, she seemed confused when I almost laughed. She kept looking into my eyes, piercing me with her stare, silently asking if I understood any of what she said. I interrupted her confusion and asked if she'd like me to explain. She did.

After I finished sharing, she broke into tears and so did I. There wasn't insight into the future with her reading, but she did hit the nail on the head, so to speak, as far as where I was right then—flip floppy.

Next was a Tarot card reading. This was fascinating. Not the reading so much, but the entire experience from beginning to end. The reader's name was Linda Moore.

Much of the beginning was very relatable to what Megan told me during my psychic reading. But when Linda reached a certain card, everything seemed to shift. At one point, her eyes synced with mine and then she said, "You're searching for information on something. You haven't yet completed that project. You will continue to search for answers until you're satisfied or have no-where else to look."

I knew instantly what she meant—my search for answers pertaining to the afterlife.

The next card represented fear. Her voice was very passionate as she spoke, "You are in fear, or have had something happen recently that has caused you much fear."

I was taken aback. How could she have known that?

There were three cards throughout that all seemed to mean the same thing. Something about figuring out what I wanted in my life, or out of my life, writing it down and wanting it, wishing it, believing in it, and knowing that it would happen. She said the Universe wanted it for me.

The third of these cards was close to the end when she stopped, stared directly into my eyes again, and whispered, "It's not normal to get three of these cards. What is it that you want out of your life, Lyn?"

I didn't hesitate. The words flew out of my mouth.

"You're making reference to materialistic items. I'm sorry, but that doesn't interest me in the least. What I want is to learn how to communicate with my fiancé who was murdered in January."

I think I surprised her.

Linda stopped reading the cards and began meditating right then. She gave me a Chip reading. She said, "He may not be here in the physical with you right now, but he's with you always. He says to tell you when you sleep at night, he's right beside you holding onto you even though you can't feel him."

She opened her eyes and stared over my right shoulder. "He says to tell you that he's right here next to you, hugging you. I can sense your guides and lots of angels all around you. All you have to do is ask for them to help you through this."

She closed her eyes again and went silent for a moment. They were filled with tears when she opened them. "He wants me to tell you this," but then she paused before finishing her statement. She took a deep breath, and then continued.

"I know you're smart enough to already know this, but you can't leave right now. You can't have suicidal thoughts and if you were to do something like that, you would ruin everything the two of you have accomplished through many lifetimes together. You would not be able to go back to him."

"I know that," I told her, "That won't happen."

"He tells me he didn't exit because he didn't want to be with you. He exited because of your contract together. It was time for him to go so that you can continue what you are supposed to do."

Did she seriously just answer a question I asked Chip only yesterday—why did you leave me?—I think she did. Her answer; one, because of this contract we have together, and two, so I could continue with what I'm supposed to do.

Linda continued, "He tells me when your exit arrives in this life, he will be the one that will hold out his hand and take you home."

Only this morning I told my sister I hoped when I died, that Chip would be the one who took me home. She couldn't have known that. Wow.

She explained that it is with *immense love* when we sign up for these contracts and go through these experiences. We don't know what it is we are going to experience when it happens, but it is with *immense love* when we agree to them.

Linda is a Master Reiki Healer. She performs regression—I thought about trying that. Maybe find out why I am the way I am in this life, why such a loner. My mother recently told me I was a different kind of child, one with no friends. She said I kept to myself mostly, but always found ways to be entertained. Regression... it'd be interesting to learn what I did in a past life to pick this one to be so different.

This was also the second time I had heard that word—*contract*. After dinner, I picked up the phone.

"About this contract thing," I said to Megan. "I'm not the only one Chip signed one with, am I? Wouldn't he have contracts or agreements with all of his loved ones?"

"I feel like the agreements, the contracts we have with people, are different. It's not the same. I do feel like he had several to be around at his passing and that while it connects all of you, it doesn't obligate any of you," Megan said.

204

"Well, the reason I asked was because Chip's mom spoke of theirs. It was a light bulb moment for me. I knew then I couldn't be the only one involved. I've also been trying hard to meditate but I always seem to fall asleep. There's been a few times where I've seen something though. Like the other day I saw a big, well dressed, gold-suited black man. He was turning around to look at me. His wife was in front of him and we were all walking into a courthouse. They were exiting an elevator."

"And then in the blink of an eye, I was watching a lady in a red SUV drive up to an entrance of an old store. It was in the middle of nowhere, on a dirt road. I watched the dust fly up everywhere and I remember clearly thinking, okay I saw that, and then bam, I was fast asleep. I don't want to go to sleep. What am I doing wrong?"

"I had a response all planned out," she said. "But then I got this. *Geez Lynnie*—did he ever call you Lynnie?—*give yourself a break.* With a smile, of course. Keep working on it. When you start to relax it's to sleep, that's normal. With more practice, relax could mean meditate or sleep. It will come."

Wow, she called me Lynnie. I couldn't believe it. Chip called me Lynnie-Poo all the time. Sometimes, he said Lynnie, but mostly it was Lynnie-Boo or Lynnie-Poo.

"Lynnie, huh? Chip had lots of nicknames for me and yes, that was one of them. Lynnie-Boo was a favorite, too. I heard it more and more there at the end. He was so cute."

"Wow, that's funny," she said. "I was getting Lynnie-Poo but dismissed it."

"Lynnie-Poo was the other one. Isn't that neat? I love it." We couldn't help but laugh. And then, I changed the subject.

"I had the strangest experience last night. I woke up around 10:30 p.m. with my stomach in knots. I ran to the bathroom and hugged the toilet. I knew I was going to throw up, I could feel it. I hung my head over and waited when the oddest thing happened. The nausea vanished. A few minutes later, I got back in bed and soon fell asleep—and then I saw her."

"All I know is that I'm supposed to find this young girl. Her head was wrapped in a bandana with purple and pink colors, with big bright stripes. I heard it and understood it—I have to take pictures of her, for her. She needs to see her angels surrounding her so she'll know she'll be all right. It was important she see the pictures to bring her peace and to understand, it was okay to leave. She was awfully sick."

"She had to be between ten and twelve years old. But I don't know any young girls. I almost wrote this off. Then I remembered how sick I felt and put two and two together. I wonder who she is. She reminded me of the little girl in the movie, *Erin Brockovich*. The young girl with a head wrap who sat next to her mom."

I was very worried about her.

Megan suggested, "I would recommend the same thing I did with Chip. He came to me in meditation and I told him to arrange to have you find me, that I couldn't help otherwise. I would say to this little girl—*set up something so that I can find you*—then when she does you'll know. The nausea is common and is probably linked to her chemo."

"Wow, I have goose bumps running through my body. Oh no, Megan. Does that mean she isn't here, in the physical world? I felt so strongly that I was supposed to find her."

"Not necessarily," Megan assured me. "It could be that she's so sick she travels back and forth. My great aunt has Alzheimer's and I think she spends more time over there than here, but still hasn't let go."

Spends more time over there than here? How is that possible? This was all weird, in a good way, but weird. I had no clue how to communicate with someone in spirit. I certainly didn't know how to help the young girl.

This was unlike anything I ever experienced before.

Why was I jumping head first into the world of spirits, expecting answers to be at my fingertips? Maybe I needed to rethink my position. Maybe I needed to close this window.

Maybe I should step back.

Chapter Thirty-Three

PICTURES

S o much for stepping back. Chip wasn't going to let that happen no matter how badly I wanted it. It was apparent we had work to do. I dove right into those pictures of the drawings on the windshield. They needed to be downloaded and seen. Besides, I was much too curious to see what they looked like up close.

I spent hours digging in, finding it hard to pry myself away. Since sharing so much of mine and Chip's new life, I felt the urge to share the drawings too. I attached a few pictures to an email and wrote to Megan, "Number 126 is my refrigerator. Check out the lighting around Chip under the Hawaii magnet on the right side. Number 132 is Scooby—so you can see what he looks like."

"The rest are the fish and a butterfly, too, that I found the other day. All of them were drawn on the windshield. Can you see faces inside the fish?"

The investigation continued. I enlarged them and saw things I had never seen before. In specific areas of the butterfly, I saw faces, people, animals, alien like creatures, a door, a gun, and much more.

Minutes later, my phone rang. It was Megan.

"I think you're right," she said. "Have you seen all of the orbs on the pictures? Dust shows up differently, as straight lines. You have perfect colored and white orbs—way cool. I do see the faces; looks like the face of a dog?! Do you see the orbs? They're beautiful."

Orbs? What were orbs? I remembered her saying that word once before. I searched to find out.

~An Orb is considered to be the soul of a once-living person or animal that appears in photographs as a spherical shaped light.~

"I'll be," I uttered, "I didn't know those were orbs. I thought it was dust on the windshield. I've enlarged all of them and I see faces in other areas."

"Yes. Orbs are spirits—so I bet you can see Chip's face in them. The colored ones are supposed to be angels. I don't remember the name of the book, but when dust particles are blown up on film they show as straight lines. When orbs are blown up, they're often faces."

"I've studied the pictures for hours, Megan. It's amazing how many dog faces I've found. In picture Number 177, I've located at least nine dogs, two of them wolves. The one fish that seems to have a hook in it—it has a Chihuahua as its face. The fish picture that isn't completed, I can see a face mask with a frown and directly next to it, a face of a dog that resembles a Lab. Do you think that might be Scooby?"

"I thought it looked just like Scooby," she agreed. "I do see all the faces."

You, too, can see the pictures also. They're posted on the page titled, "Gallery", located at www.LynRagan.com.

Chapter Thirty-Four

HE'S THIRD
PARTYING AGAIN

had made it. I had finally climbed that tall mountain, high up into the cirrus clouds of mystical wonder. I was living in a world all by myself, but it was one of awareness unlike anything I'd ever known. I had a secret I knew no one would ever believe.

Chip wasn't dead!

He was far from it. He was painting a picture unlike any designed in the history of the world. Well, in my world anyway. Sure I was crawling slowly through the depths of despair, but by the same token, I marveled at his communications from a faraway land. No matter how badly he confused me, I had a new belief. An unshakable new belief.

Life continues past physical death.

The picture, the larger definition of life, was grander than my mind was allowed to touch. Wrapping my head around it was impossible but leave it to me to try. My zodiac sign was a goat and those shoes were filled proudly with one small exception—I was a *stubborn* goat.

If I didn't understand how something worked, I studied it for hours, days, even weeks to make it logical. And sometimes, I had to let it go in order to see something new.

Incredibly, when I met with that something new, it always seemed bigger than the gift before it. Take today for example.

A day that changed my life. A day I repeatedly used as a guiding tool when I felt down or when I felt doubt.

It happened on a bright, sunny Wednesday morning. It wasn't going to be a busy day at work, so I decided to take the longer route and enjoy my commute. I was in no hurry.

After settling in and putting my belongings away, I heard the pitter-patter of footsteps walking across the floor down the long hallway. Someone was coming to see me.

It was Dana, a co-worker and dear friend. She immediately sat across from me and requested my full, undivided attention. I could tell she was shaken and a bit nervous. Instantly, I became concerned.

"Are you okay? What's wrong?" I asked her.

She stared hard into my eyes but remained silent. About the time I was getting up to walk over, she spoke.

"I swear I'm not crazy or anything," I dared not break our connection, "But I think Chip came to visit me last night."

My heart plummeted to the floor.

A smile so large creeped across my face. My concern for her well-being vanished when instant and anxious energy devoured my essence. I was all ears.

"First, I have to describe the overwhelming feeling of peacefulness I felt. It was almost like winning the lottery. Like there were no worries or concerns. It felt like everything had been lifted off of my shoulders. It was the most intense feeling of peace I'd ever felt in my life. And it felt so real."

She took a deep breath.

"We were walking into a two story house, you and me. It was your house, but it wasn't your house. We walked through the doorway and you turned to ask me if I could see them. I asked, 'See who?' And you said, 'All of these spirits.' I looked around and then said, 'No, I don't see anyone.'"

"We stood there talking to each other in the parlor when Chip appeared in front of me. I was staring at him. I couldn't take my eyes off of him. Then you turned to walk toward a corner in the living room to go and talk to those spirits. There seemed to be a big party going on."

"I know Chip and I were talking back and forth but our mouths weren't moving, and I don't remember any of the conversation. I do know it was about you though. He would watch you as we talked about you."

"I stood there in front of him and I said, 'I can't believe I can see you so clearly and so well. I can't believe you are sitting there. You're dead.'"

"He laughed. Everything in the dream from the beginning to the end was gray except for him. He wore a white tee-shirt and blue shorts. Sitting on the corner of a bench with his elbows resting on his knees, he was laughing, with his head tilted back."

"Then he got serious and said, 'I am okay here.' He looked toward you again and told me, 'You have to make her understand that what she feels, what she hears, and what she sees is real.' I said, 'Okay.'"

"I turned around and walked out the front door. The only thing I noticed was how gray everything was still. I walked through tall grass and then stood next to a tree when I freaked out. I realized I didn't say goodbye."

"I tried to find the house to go back, but it was gone. Then you walked up and asked, 'What's wrong?' I was crying uncontrollably. I told you, 'He came all this way to visit me and I didn't even say goodbye.'"

"You grabbed me and hugged me and said, 'It's okay. I talk to him all the time. I will tell him for you.'"

"And then, I woke up."

My smile was irremovable. Our eyes were still locked, but I sensed she wasn't as thrilled as I. She was deeply disturbed and extremely serious.

"What I know, Lyn, is that I *have* to make you understand. I'm not supposed to just tell you. He wants me to *make* you understand."

She sat, unmoving, and patiently waited for me to respond.

"I got it." I blurted.

"Good," she bounced up, "Now make sure you tell him I said goodbye so he doesn't come back! I don't want to go through *that* again."

I sat in awe for the longest. Dazed. I couldn't believe any of it, yet I knew every bit of it was real. I had been given a new secret. One that would become my lifeline when confusion set in.

When I questioned if it was his words I heard, it was. When I questioned if I could feel him, I could. When I questioned if the dreams were real, they were.

It was time to believe he was real.

I literally skipped around in a big fluffy, cumulus cloud of delight. I danced through work and drove home without a tear in sight. I cleaned the dishes, took care of the kids, and before dark approached, I walked outside and made a call—to Chip's mom.

At one point in our conversation I walked inside. When I turned the corner, I froze in place. I was stunned. Sitting on top of the kitchen counter was a single key. And nothing else.

I went completely blank for a brief moment.

"Char," I took a deep breath, "There's a key lying here on my counter. One little silver key—and I don't know where it came from."

I took the key through the house checking it in the doors,

but it didn't fit anywhere. Then I remembered something. Several months ago, Chip had placed the key to his house inside the car door.

In the dark now, I walked outside. There wasn't a key in sight, only loose change. I had no other recourse but to acknowledge that the magically appearing key had traveled from my locked up car and was placed on the kitchen counter ... mysteriously.

Did I dare suggest Chip did this?

Absolutely. Don't ask me how he did it because I don't know. All I can say is his fascination with *keys* was a continued marvel.

After the mystery was solved, I leaned across the counter and watched my little Miss Angel hop all over her big bed. It was the funniest sight. She looked so cute ... playing with someone I couldn't see.

My heart was filled with warmth today. Both Angel and I had been kissed, again, with Chip's love from that other side.

What an incredible day...

Chapter Thirty-Five

HAPPY BIRTHDAY

I 've been thinking," I told Megan, "About the three fish pictures. The day I noticed them was the day I had my psychic reading with you. The more I study them, well, tell me if this makes sense, okay?"

"Okay, go," said Megan.

"The one to the furthest right is Chip—inside this picture I see a small dog face leading the way. This could either be the Underdog reference or a Chihuahua symbolizing my Charlie who died last year. Either way, I think it belongs to Chip."

"The fish in the middle I think refers to you—there are no pictures of faces, of dogs or anything. It simply looks like a female with soft clouds floating in the form of a fish. The last one to the left, I think refers to me."

"Inside this fish is a mask, the famous tragedy mask, and a picture of a Lab that I think is Scooby. He's letting me know it's a tragedy he's not here for Scoob."

"It's uncanny that two of these fish have other animals in them but the one in the middle does not. Is this a message? Maybe a message where the two of you are guiding me or directing me in the right direction?"

Megan thought for a moment and then shared, "When I look at your pictures I see the same things you do," she said. "I have a different take on the tragedy mask, see what resonates for you. Scooby is a ham and all the world is a stage—divine comedy or divine tragedy—that you can make of it whatever you want. I do feel like it's a nudge in the right direction. This happened after the car door locks, correct? You needed something concrete that you could look at, right?"

"Yes," I answered. "I think the fish pictures were right around the same time as the door locks. Wow, I never thought of that. So he was giving me something else, like you said, concrete to look at. I wonder now if the car went crazy because of the fish pictures—maybe it was all that energy he left in the car after he painted them on the windshield."

Proof of the Afterlife.

It was staring me in the face, literally. Physical proof. It wasn't telepathy. It wasn't a song. It wasn't a knock on the counter, or a butterfly flapping its sweet delicate wings. It wasn't a beautiful floating feather, or a coin with the year of his birth. It wasn't a set of numbers, like 123, the day he died.

No, it was real physical proof.

Pictures drawn by a dead man.

It never dawned on me to look at his drawings as proof of life after death. I wasn't sure what he wanted me to do with his artwork… if anything. Maybe they were simply a gift to prove he was real. Maybe he drew them so I'd stop dismissing him. Maybe he drew them so I'd stop questioning his communications.

Whatever the reason, I treasured each and every one. He had pulled me in. I was hooked. His number one fan. I would later become his advocate. Exposing him like a radiant, glowing, pearl.

The next morning, however, he uncovered me. It was his birthday, yet he felt the need to gift me with a trip to Hawaii.

I was at work, looking around, trying to place all of the people around me. I recognized a few old faces but there were lots of new ones too. I was their supervisor.

I was giving direction and getting a little annoyed at a few for slacking off. Standing at the front door gazing out, I heard a man walk in from the back of the building.

"The bridge is about to close for the next few hours," he hollered. "So if you want to get something to eat, you need to go now." Everyone dashed away.

I didn't seem too interested in their attempt to rush off for lunch though. Instead, I opened the front door and stepped outside. I gasped for air.

I melted into splendor. The grass was so plush and so green, it looked velvety smooth. And it covered hills upon hills as far as I could see.

The trees were meticulously placed in perfect harmony bearing several colors of green. It was gorgeous. I stared out soaking in the majestic goddess herself; mother nature.

When I turned my head, I saw a sidewalk on top of an incline. I decided to follow the path to it. A male voice could be heard yelling for me, but I ignored him. I rushed to the sidewalk and then took a look to the right. When I did, I saw Chip walking toward me.

He was skipping. Taking extra-big steps. He looked so happy and his smile was extra-large. When he was close enough, his eyes plunged into mine.

Instantly, I saw what he was wearing; blue board shorts and sandals. No shirt. He planted his arm around me and gently turned me, guiding us to the end of the railing in the opposite direction.

I gazed out into a beautiful manicured pasture, admiring the stillness of its green allure. I breathed in a deep breath of crisp air and then glanced down. I gasped again.

Lying in front of me was a gorgeous mother Bengal tiger. I

sensed she was a little slow, a little ill maybe. She was walking
around in a circle. On her third attempt, I noticed she had
three cute little babies.

"Oh, they're adorable," I said. "Hey, are we in the wild?"

"No darlin, we're in Hawaii."

Chip's chin rested on top of my shoulder. He leaned his face
closer to mine and directed my attention to the right a little
farther. He told me to look through the mountainous hills of
trees in front of us.

"Do you see that light that's on directly through those trees
right there?" He was pointing now.

"Yes," I replied.

"That's where our little coffee shop is, sweetie," he said.

My eyes flickered open as I became aware. I lay still, unable
to move, in complete awe.

"Wow, you took me to Hawaii," I whispered, happily.

I was more in love with Chip than yesterday... if that was
even possible. He was always finding a way to knock me off
my feet.

May 5, 2008
Monday — Chip's Birthday

No work today. It was Chip's birthday. If he were here, we
would have been long gone on a road trip to south Florida. We
loved to escape and our mini-vacations were a great way to do
that.

My sister arrived the day before from Fort Lauderdale to
share in Chip's celebration. At first, I thought I would be alone
and I was okay with that. I had easily planned a wonderful
morning at the beach to watch the sun rise. Time had changed
that plan. My sister and Chip's mom were joining me. It was
going to be a great day—I could feel it.

Flowers and balloons already purchased for his birthday, we were out the door at 5:15 a.m. heading to the beach. Forty-five minutes later, we stopped at Starbucks for coffee and then drove to the end of Atlantic Boulevard.

Upon reaching a turnaround point, I couldn't for the life of me remember which way to go. Always the passenger with Chip, I never paid attention to the roads. I saw no where to park and even if there was, there'd be no privacy. So I drove us out and stopped at the next light.

I sat for a minute and according to my sister, I said, "Darlin, which way do we go?" Suddenly, I made a right-hand turn and then stopped at the next stop sign. After glancing down the road, I said, "This is it."

Following along a wooden privacy fence, I was sure I picked a great spot to park. I shut the car off and from the back seat, my sister asked, "Lyn, do you see what you parked next to?"

I hadn't. I turned to look out the window and to my complete surprise, the fence was covered in designs of sea life; dolphins, fish, starfish, etc. Unbeknownst to me, I had parked right beside a dolphin. I laughed.

"This is exactly where we're supposed to be," I said.

We unpacked the car and loaded up to hike to the beach. It was around 6:30 a.m. and the light of day was beginning to show. The sun would be coming up soon. We sat and gazed out and took in the beauty of the loud but peaceful water.

A few minutes later, I decided to snap a few pictures. Barely able to make it out, what was captured was something other than the ocean and the sky. It looked almost ghost-like.

"Chip's definitely here," I whispered.

At seven o'clock we let the balloons float up and watched as they climbed the sky. I battled the tears—I was determined this would be a day of celebration, not one filled with sorrow.

Chip would have loved this, I thought quietly. It was a beautiful moment watching the balloons disappear, but also a sad one too. This was where we loved to be, on the beach, and without him here—it felt unreal.

Once the sun rose, the time had come to toss the silky carnations into the ocean and sing *Happy Birthday* to Chip. Afterwards, we sat in our chairs, speechless, and watched the brilliant orange sun, rise above the water. I refused to move. My head was full, yet it felt incredibly empty. The scenery was a perfect mixture for a hypnotic setting.

"Lyn, did you see that?" my sister shouted, pointing out toward the water.

"See what?"

"The dolphin. Right there," she shouted out.

"Oh wow! There he is," I jumped up excitedly. Again and again the dolphin crested the tip of the white water. He was marvelous. And beautiful. But that wasn't the end of the surprise.

Two more dolphins appeared. They followed the same path as the first. Mama and baby, following Papa. It was amazing to observe. As many times as Chip and I had watched the sun rise together, we had never experienced seeing dolphins. I knew he had something to do with this. He had to. Chip knew how much I loved dolphins—he bought me a pearl ring in the Florida Keys—my first dolphin ring—he knew I loved them.

We stood in silence, all three of us, enjoying our front row seats until the dolphins disappeared into the distance. An elderly man had appeared and I noticed he wore a breathing apparatus. He seemed to be a sweet old man.

"Hello," my sister said.

"Good morning," his deep voice replied. "Did you see the

dolphins?"

"Yes, sir. We certainly did. Do you see them here often?"

"No. You're lucky if you see something like that maybe once or twice a year. You've been blessed," he said.

I leaned in toward sister and whispered, "Well. Now isn't that interesting?" She smirked, knowing exactly what I meant.

What a perfect choice of words he had spoken. *You've been blessed.* They were dangling in the air, like bait on a hook. There we were, wishing Chip a happy birthday and there he was, sending *us* gifts instead.

It was so like him.

Chip had to be the star. He loved being the center of attention, hogging it up all the time. I wouldn't have it any other way. If that's what he wanted to do, he could have it all. I loved everything he did.

We spent the rest of the day honoring his birthday and sharing his favorite dinner; barbeque ribs and potato salad. My sister flew home afterwards and I planned to use the evening to study. The pictures I took on the beach were tearing at my curiosity. I needed to see them.

It didn't take long to witness a few ghost-like Beings. Whatever they were, they seemed to be jumping *into* the photos. It was clear as day.

I decided to share and wrote a short note to Megan.

"Happy Birthday to Chip Oney. He's forty-two today."

"We celebrated his birthday at the beach this morning. I snapped a bunch of pictures and a few are quite interesting. Can I ask you a couple questions? If I can capture these faces from this other side, who are they? Do I know these people? And... why are they all around me?"

Before bed I jumped back online.

She had responded. "These pictures are amazing. He was

there, your loved ones were there and I think his deceased loved ones were there for the party too. I feel like the many, many faces are a mix. Some you know, some he knows, some come just because the light is on."

I wasn't certain what she meant so I wrote back.

"The light is on? Do you mean my light or his, or both?"

"Your light is on," she wrote. "And from the other side, they flock to the light."

Chapter Thirty-Six

BUTTERFLY

F or a time, the pictures became an outlet for my sorrow. I spent days, weeks, searching inside of them every night. I looked for different objects, faces, and animals; whatever I could find. It soared me into oblivion.

And the dreams. They came quite often, too. I couldn't help but be in awe. Most days I got right out of bed, smiled, made my coffee, and scooted to the computer to document them. I was still sad, but not as sad as I was that first day. It took months getting comfortable with the truth—Chip wasn't dead.

One night, I asked him a question. I was outside staring up at the dark sky, searching for the stars. The words just leaped off my tongue.

"Why didn't we get married?"

There was no answer though. I didn't hear a thing. No song, no phrases, no thoughts, there was nothing. So I went to bed. The next thing I knew...

I was sitting on a large brown, luxuriant, sectional sofa watching TV. Chip was sitting next to me; I was sprawled out across him feeling very relaxed and comfortable. I sensed my sister sitting across from us, too.

A commercial was on and I looked toward the kitchen. It was disgusting in there. Dishes were piled up in the sink, on the counter, and the garbage was over flowing. It was messy and not the way I lived. I felt the need to clean so I got up and headed in. Sister came too.

"Hey girls, who's going to cook us something to eat?" Chip shouted.

I turned and answered, "I'm going to fix us macaroni and ham. Is that good?" We loved that stuff and made it at least once a week. He gave me his charming smile and nodded, yes.

My cell phone rang abruptly, distracting me. I saw it sitting on the counter facing the dining room, or laundry room. I couldn't be sure. I rushed over to pick it up and looked at the caller ID. It said, "MatureOne".

At first, it seemed the name was used to disguise someone. I heard a lady's voice and shockingly, she knew who I was. She then started talking about a church in the area.

At the same time, Chip's phone rang and I watched him walk into the kitchen to answer it. He smiled big, melting my heart, and then turned and walked away.

"Would you like to attend our church? It's located on the north side of town?" the female voice asked.

"No, I go to the church on this side of town. But thank you for asking." I hung the phone up and walked to the sink. I wondered why I had said that to her—I didn't attend a church on any side of town.

The next thing I knew, I was in the back yard with Chip. I didn't recognize a thing. But it didn't matter. My focus was directed on him. As long as I was with him I didn't care where we were. I walked closer, grabbed his hands into mine, and looked up into his eyes.

"I want to marry you. Right now," I boldly said.

"We can't in this life, my love," he answered gently.

"I know we can't. But I still want to marry you." I cradled his hands and held them tightly against my chest. My head dropped and I stared at the ground below, disappointed. My heart ached. I wanted to marry him, right then.

He reached under my chin, lifted my head, and stared into my eyes. "We're already married, sweetie. And we'll spend all of eternity together," he softly whispered.

I melted... into his eyes of blue.

My eyes reluctantly opened.

I instantly felt my arms stretched across the bed, but I laid still, adjusting to my awakeness.

"That felt so real," I voiced out loud.

Instead of wrapping his arms around me, he was wrapping me up in his love. I didn't have his physical love anymore, but I sure as heck had his spiritual love. I was in heaven.

About getting married—we didn't want to rush into it. We both knew we would marry someday, but I was more adamant than him. We didn't need a piece of paper to show us we loved each other like a husband and wife.

The sad part though—I would have been fine if we never married. I didn't want another failed marriage. To do something different, something that felt right and felt good, I thought it made more sense not to marry than to screw it all up with a piece of paper. But now?

I wished I would have said *yes* when he asked me to marry him in Georgia one afternoon. But no, not me. I had to be the sensible one. I had to be the one to look out for our future, to protect him, to protect me. Today, there's no making sense of why I didn't marry him then. I certainly wasn't living in the moment. Instead, I was living in the future.

We were supposed to complete a few tasks we set in place too. One, get life insurance policies in case something ever happened. Our goal was to make sure each of us were taken care of in the event one of us died.

And number two, open a new IRA account. We were planning our future and retirement was key. Two days before he was murdered, we made a plan. There was to be no more procrastination. I made the appointment to meet our insurance agent on Friday and then on Saturday, we would head to the bank to open the IRA. We were also going to put a down payment on a house.

We found two homes actually. One of them would be ours. We were so excited to start a new life together. Sadly, someone else had Chip's fate in their hands. We procrastinated too long—there was no IRA and there was no life insurance.

If hindsight was twenty-twenty, there would have been both, and there would have been a marriage. Without that piece of paper, a significant other has no say in matters concerning a loved one who passes.

If I've learned anything from Chip's death, I've learned to cover the bases. It's never too early to discuss the future. It's never too early to draw up a will. A will that clearly defines the distribution of assets. It's the right thing to do to protect the ones you love. There are no lengths people will go to when death knocks down that door.

That dream-visit certainly brought back a lot of memories of procrastination, but it also carried a beautiful message.

We're already married and we'll spend eternity together. I crawled out of bed to start the new day. I had an engagement planned. A phone call with Megan. I took my time waking up and prepared myself for what I was about to share.

Something spectacular happened the night before.

I started the conversation, "I had the hardest time falling asleep last night. Every time I felt I was going out, I heard noises in the bedroom like someone was walking around. When I opened my eyes there was nothing there. Eventually, I accepted it may be Chip and finally, I drifted off."

"I don't know if I was asleep or if I was awake when this

happened. I can't even begin to differentiate. At some point during the night, I opened my eyes and when I did, Chip got out of the bed and walked toward the bathroom. I didn't see his head or his legs, only a white tee-shirt draping his body. I watched him walk slowly to the bathroom."

"It was like no time had passed and nothing had changed. And like I did a hundred times before, I watched him for a moment and then closed my eyes and went back to sleep. I didn't recognize that he was dead and not here anymore. If I would have, I could have stopped him and talked to him. But I had no clue."

"That's the hardest thing for me to understand, Megan. He's visited so many others and talks to them, including you. But with me, I get no visit that lets me feel or know he isn't here anymore. He keeps me in the past. I don't know, I don't understand why he does this. Why doesn't he allow me to talk to him?"

"In John Edwards' books," she said, "He talks about when his mother passed. He told her to come to other people rather than him. Because they knew each other so well, he would second guess anything that came through directly to him. That's what I think is happening for you. If you did get a direct message, you may dismiss it as hopeful thinking."

"Chip comes through to me and to others with clear messages of what's happening now so you can't second guess them. For last night, I feel like he's reassuring you he is here now, with you. With the walking around the bed, getting up in the middle of the night, the pictures from the beach and the fish on your windshield; he's here now with you. I feel like it's not so much about the past, but dissuading any thoughts you have about being alone. Because you are not."

Because you're not alone… I was astounded. I didn't see

that coming. Did I seriously refuse to look outside the box? I should have seen that. All of that. I knew I wasn't alone.

I felt so silly.

"Thank you, Megan. That makes perfect sense. I don't know why I don't think of it this way when I go through it. I know it's all real. I need to stop thinking so much and just be grateful he's with me."

"Before I forget, I want to share more pictures with you. Chip's been busy again. He's drawn more. We now have a cute little squirrel and a funky looking clown face. On the rearview mirror, he's drawn a puppy with a bow. And right below the puppy is a pretty dolphin. Blessed am I, no doubt about it. And I know it."

I attached the photos as we chatted.

"I think I'm starting to scare myself," I told her. "Are the things in these pictures normal? Am I okay here? They're basically here to say hi and none of them, whatever they are, want to harm me, right?"

"This is amazing!" she shouted. "Nothing bad, just amazing. There is so much. There is life after death, and those that have passed from violence are still just as, if not more, full of love and possibility."

"Story for you," she continued. "Our puppy loves to eat wood. We've gotten about sixteen inches of snow today and the wood fire's going. He's eating all the wood in the house. Right before your call, my sweetie yelled, 'Megan, we named our dog the wrong name. Instead of Sean, he should be called Chip or Chipper.' There you go. Another hello."

"Oh how neat is that? I love that!" We laughed together.

"Hey, you didn't tell me if I'm okay here with all of these spirits."

"Totally," she said. "You are fine. There's nothing ominous

around you."

Our call ended, but my curiosity did not. She used a word I hadn't heard before, *ominous*. I didn't want to look dumb so I looked it up.

Ominous—menacing, threatening; also, of or being an omen. Especially an evil one.

In other words, there was nothing menacing or threatening going on. There was no omen, especially an evil one, around me. That had me feeling much better and made it easier to finish out the work day and get ready for later. I had plans. Chip's mom invited me over for dinner.

When it was time to go however, I wasn't feeling well. My stomach was in knots and I knew I couldn't rush over and eat dinner. I needed to rest. Maybe close my eyes. And pray I didn't throw up all over the place.

Scooby was off in a training camp—my only responsibility at the moment was Angel. I took her outside to potty and then fed her. I then laid back on the sofa, kicked my feet up on the coffee table, and closed my eyes.

The back door was left opened. The weather wasn't scorching hot yet and I loved the fresh air. The air conditioner kicked on outside sounding like a distant waterfall. The hum was calming and it helped me feel more comfortable.

Suddenly, I was looking at an old steel bridge in front of me. It was silver with red markings painted all over. I could distinctly hear the water running by loudly, underneath the bridge as I walked across it.

Somewhere in the middle I decided to look over the edge. The stream was traveling fast, downhill. The wind was surfing off of the water; I could feel its chill. It was a little cool, a little crisp. "I wish I had my sweater," I said.

Up ahead there was a dirt road at the end of the bridge. I followed it with my eyes until it veered off to the right and disappeared. When I reached the end of the bridge, I stopped. Someone was standing on the left side of the road.

It was a man. He was alone. Standing there staring at me. The water was traveling louder so I knew I was getting closer. But an uneasiness quickly came over me. I couldn't move.

I stood still. Watching the man. Wanting him to move across before I proceeded. In my head, he was supposed to cross that road. So I didn't budge. But neither did he.

We stood motionless, staring at each other. And then he did something strange. He smiled. "Is that Chip?" I asked.

I squinted my eyes, inspecting intently. As soon as I did, darkness prevailed. Suddenly, the sofa could be felt underneath me. I remained still and kept my eyes tightly closed.

And then a male's voice whispered. .

It wasn't a whisper derived from telepathy. It was a whisper I heard with my physical self. Someone literally leaned over my left shoulder, close to my ear, and slowly—whispered.

"B.u.t.t.e.r.f.l.y — b.u.t.t.e.r.f.l.y — b.u.t.t.e.r.f.l.y"

On the third *butterfly*, my eyes popped.

I was staring directly at the clock on top of the TV and that's when I realized I must have dozed off... for five minutes. It didn't feel like I was sleeping though. It felt too real. Too alive. I hadn't experienced anything like it before.

It seemed anytime I questioned if Chip was real, he squashed my stubbornness and did something different to make me understand how wrong I was.

This *butterfly* communication changed everything. For the first time, I didn't carry a shadow of doubt. I didn't only believe he was communicating from the other side—I *knew* he was.

I also knew butterflies symbolized transformation. The butterfly was the same Being as the caterpillar—just different … like him.

Yes, Chip was alive. And by God, he was making sure I understood just how much.

Chapter Thirty-Seven

MAGICAL MOMENTS

"What's the most memorable moment you shared with Chip?" my sister asked. He'd been gone three days. I stared blankly out the window feeling more lost than I'd ever felt in my life. I was being led everywhere. Like a passenger going through the motions.

We were sitting in the car waiting for a copy of Chip's obituary. I didn't have a lot of strength and engaging in conversation was the last thing I wanted to do. At the same time I knew she was only trying to help. Her heart was crying for me and she hadn't a clue how to assist me. Her question though. It was too easy to answer.

"Every single moment. I can't possibly give you only one."

How could I pick only one moment? Especially at a time of such devastation. A few months later, she asked that same question but this time, I was in a different state. It was Chip's birthday and I proudly shared my answer.

"When he told me he was *in love* with me," I said.

It was a Friday night in the month of April. Chip had called on his way to pick me up. "Let's get *real* food tonight," he said. "How about seafood?" He knew my weakness, seafood. But wondering what our dress code needed to be, I had to ask.

"What are you wearing? Are we going casual or dress up?"

"I'm wearing my new Tommy Bahama orange shirt and my new shorts we bought in West Palm," he said.

I couldn't help it. I laughed. He was so darn cute.

"Do you have your new Tommy Bahama sandals on, too?"

"Of course I do," he said, laughing. He was such a goober.

I had to hurry off the phone to change clothes. I threw on the dress he bought me and changed my shoes. I didn't expect us to go out again that week, but I adored the plan.

He wouldn't tell me where we were going. He said he wanted it to be a surprise. A long time ago he insisted I broaden my horizons and was always taking me places I hadn't been. He made me feel like a true queen.

We wound up at a seafood restaurant close to the beach. We never drank, but that night we both enjoyed a margarita. By the time we finished dinner, we were feeling a little tipsy.

We left feeling extremely full. There wasn't room for our usual weekend coffee, but we didn't want to go home either. Chip insisted we go for a ride, so he drove us toward Mayport.

We were having such a great time; laughing, joking around, talking, laughing more, when out of the blue he slammed me with a surprise.

"I am *so* in love with you!" he said boisterously.

Instantly, the world came to a halt and time had stopped. Everything stood still. He grabbed my hand and pulled it up as I watched his lips gently caress my skin. I was stunned. My heart was beating fast. I felt queasy. Dizzy. Like I was inside of a movie living a real life fantasy—watching a fairy tale.

No man ever said those words before.

Not that way. We told each other a hundred times a day we loved each other. But this was different.

That moment marked the change of *us*. We changed. We sailed from one realm into another. It swallowed us up and allowed us to experience a brand new journey filled with a love unlike any we experienced before. We never knew what hit us.

It just happened. And neither of us fought it.

And then came an experience I'd never forget...

It was an early morning on a cloudy summer's day. Time became nothing but at the same time, it was everything. I was as light as a feather, far out in the universe somewhere, when life as I knew it, changed.

There was music. And vibrations. And colors galore in the background of space. My astral body was embraced, cradled like a new born babe. There were a thousand harps, ringing chimes, violins, and exquisite tones of a thousand angels humming like a graceful orchestra.

At the same time, Chip's essence was flowing freely through the galaxy telling me a story. One I'd never forget.

Baby doll, I am always with you, always letting you know I'm there. I may have left the physical world, but I will never leave you. Look around. What do you see?

You notice me everywhere, right? I haven't left, darlin. And I never will. I'm always telling you I love you. So please stop worrying.

I know you're fighting me when it comes to writing our story. You're a good warrior, Lynnie-Poo, I'll give you that. But I'm much better at this than you. You know I'll win.

(His loud laugh wrapped all around me).

I know it's hard, darlin. I know you don't want to relive my physical death. But you have to know this—that day was only the beginning of something wonderful. I know you can't see it, but trust me, it's bigger than you and me combined. I'll help. I promise. Always look for my signs.

Would it help if I shared a brief summary about our book and how it will help so many? Yes? All right.

You call our language, "communicating with the afterlife," right? Well, we call it "following Inner Voice." To the human, inner voice means listening to your gut. But over here, Inner

Voice is mightier than that. Inner Voice energy actually connects human to spirit.

When we use this unique language, Inner Voice, also known as IV, we're able to transcend through all time and space. In simple terms, it's a method of communication and a language humans can understand that isn't limited to human words.

Energy begets energy. By accelerating the IV energy, we can do anything we want... within reason of course. And we can do it much faster than the speed of light. We use a myriad of symbols, energies, signs, and thoughts, all projected using both of our IV energies—yours and mine. We're always connected and we're always communicating.

Contrary to popular belief, darlin, it isn't that hard for us to leave signs. We do it all the time. The problem with our signs not being seen however, lies mostly within the recipient.

Death is not the end of who we are. Our love will never die. This is the message we will share. We have made our transitions here on this side, but we never leave our loved ones behind, ever. We are always close, and we know what's going on with our dear ones.

So what will we share with our readers? Well, first we'll tell them to be watchful and always pay attention. We'll tell them it could be their loved one who sent them that rainbow, or that feather, or that coin, or that perfect stone.

We'll tell them it could be their loved one who sent them that familiar song they heard on the radio, or that special dream in which their special one appeared happy, healthy, and strong. Or they may see a number, or a set of numbers, that symbolize a birthday, a passing, or a time. Like our number... 1,2,3. You know that wasn't a coincidence, right?

We'll tell them they may also see a beautiful creature their loved one adored; such as a butterfly, or a ladybug, or a

238

special kind of bird. Or maybe they'll see a turtle, or a deer, or a fish that suddenly appears and reminds them of their special one. Or they may smell the wonderful aroma of their loved one's favorite flower or scent.

We'll tell them to question everything. Even the gentle touches they may feel on their face and then excuse it for a simple breeze. They should know we send these messages and signs with the deepest of Cosmic Love.

We'll also let them know how our love on this side vibrates with the energy of their love. And when they think of us, ask for us, reach out for us, we're already there. We never left.

We'll tell them they can learn anew. We'll show them how they can retrain their thoughts and beliefs. And how this will allow for the opportunity to know that it is possible to hear us, to see us, and to feel us. This is important, Lynnie. This is their awakening too.

Where will you come in? Well, darlin, you understand all of this now. You've experienced it firsthand. They will have similar questions like yours, and you will have the compassion to understand their grief, their awakening, and then share in their enlightenment that follows.

Why? Because this is your assignment now.

So when you ask what you can possibly share with the world, here is your answer. This. All of this.

One more thing before you go back. We'd like for you to include an S.O.S. for us. A universal message of sorts.

You ready? Okay, don't forget this. Here it is...

"I love you. I am not gone. I am here, right beside you. You may not see me, but I am here. I'll never leave you."

"I am everywhere. I am in your house, your car, your job, your life, your thoughts... I am in your heart... trust me, I am here. And, I love you."

I can't stop lovin' you, my darlin.
That's the key to everything. Love.

Our love lives forever.

To be continued…

You make me want to dream with eyes wide open...

September 23, 2010

Two and a half years after Chip's death, the man who shot and killed him was arrested and charged with *First Degree Murder*. His trial wouldn't begin until January 23, 2012, exactly four years to the date of that tragic day.

Five days later, a jury of his peers found him *guilty,* and in April of 2012, the killer was sentenced to life in prison without the possibility of parole.

ABOUT THE AUTHOR

Lyn Ragan knew at the age of fourteen that she would write a book one day. She subscribed to *True Crime* and *True Detective*, reading each edition faithfully while plotting her fiction novel she never wrote. Twenty-five years later, she met the love of her life never thinking she'd be involved in a real-life crime. After her fiancé's murder, she followed his guidance by way of ADC's, (After Death Communications). From the other side, Chip insisted she write their story. Following her struggles with grief and added defiance, she reluctantly gave in. Through music, Chip communicated the title and cover art for this book. The song by Wham, *Wake Me Up Before You Go-Go,* inspired the title and *Stairway To Heaven,* by Led Zeppelin, inspired the cover.

While writing her first novel, Lyn was introduced to the spiritual arts of energy work. She pursued meditation intently and went on to study Reiki Healing, Auric Energies, and Chakra Balancing. She later used her studies to become a professional Aura Photographer, an Ordained Minister, a Children's Book author, and a publisher. Lyn enjoys sharing her afterlife experiences with Chip and hopes their story will help shed new light on continuing relationships with loved ones passed. She lives in Atlanta with her fur-kids, Scooby, Chipper, and Scooter. You can find Lyn on her website, *www.LynRagan.com,* and Facebook on *WakeMeUpBook.*

Made in the USA
Middletown, DE
16 October 2018